T0277608

Cambridge Elements ≡

Elements in Women Theatre Makers
edited by
Elaine Aston
Lancaster University
Melissa Sihra
Trinity College Dublin

WOMEN MAKING SHAKESPEARE IN THE TWENTY-FIRST CENTURY

Kim Solga
Western University

CAMBRIDGE
UNIVERSITY PRESS

Shaftesbury Road, Cambridge CB2 8EA, United Kingdom

One Liberty Plaza, 20th Floor, New York, NY 10006, USA

477 Williamstown Road, Port Melbourne, VIC 3207, Australia

314–321, 3rd Floor, Plot 3, Splendor Forum, Jasola District Centre,
New Delhi – 110025, India

103 Penang Road, #05–06/07, Visioncrest Commercial, Singapore 238467

Cambridge University Press is part of Cambridge University Press & Assessment,
a department of the University of Cambridge.

We share the University's mission to contribute to society through the pursuit of
education, learning and research at the highest international levels of excellence.

www.cambridge.org
Information on this title: www.cambridge.org/9781009500883

DOI: 10.1017/9781009064507

First published 2024

A catalogue record for this publication is available from the British Library.

ISBN 978-1-009-50088-3 Hardback
ISBN 978-1-009-07348-6 Paperback
ISSN 2634-2391 (online)
ISSN 2634-2383 (print)

Cambridge University Press & Assessment has no responsibility for the persistence
or accuracy of URLs for external or third-party internet websites referred to in this
publication and does not guarantee that any content on such websites is, or will
remain, accurate or appropriate.

Women Making Shakespeare in the Twenty-First Century

Elements in Women Theatre Makers

DOI: 10.1017/9781009064507
First published online: June 2024

Kim Solga
Western University
Author for correspondence: Kim Solga, ksolga@uwo.ca

Abstract: This Element examines why women makers from equity-owed communities (Indigenous, of colour, Deaf, disabled, trans, and non-binary communities, among others) choose to work with Shakespeare and his contemporaries at a moment in time when theatres around the world are striving toward equity, inclusion, diversity, and decolonization. It details and explores these creators' processes to learn from them about how to transform plays we know all too well as patriarchy-affirming, ableist, and often racist into vehicles for community storytelling and models for radically inclusive and difference-centred ways of making.

This Element also has a video abstract: www.cambridge.org/EWTM-Solga

Keywords: decolonization, intersectionality, creation practices, women artists, Shakespeare

ISBNs: 9781009500883 (HB), 9781009073486 (PB), 9781009064507 (OC)
ISSNs: 2634-2391 (online), 2634-2383 (print)

Contents

In loving memory of Catherine Silverstone

1 Introduction: Women Making Shakespeare Now

It's a wintry evening in Toronto, March 2019. I've taken students from my history of performance theory seminar to see *Prince Hamlet*, created by Why Not Theatre. Dawn Jani Birley plays Horatio, who in this adaptation is our storyteller. She seamlessly code-switches between her character in the story and her character *as* the story: she exchanges dialogue in American Sign Language (ASL) with her best friend Hamlet (Christine Horne) while also narrating the whole play in ASL, in her own translation. Later, in interviews with Birley, with director Ravi Jain, and with Why Not co-artistic director Miriam Fernandes, I will learn just how complex, fraught, and generative the process of building this play was, and I will learn about Birley's commitment to a very specific form of intersectionality (see Section 3). Right now, though, I'm riveted like my students as we experience a familiar story in a very unfamiliar register. At the intermission, one student tells me her high school did *Julius Caesar*, not *Hamlet*; this is her first one. She's a bit worried because it's not traditional, conventional – "correct." I tell her it's the best first *Hamlet* anyone could ever encounter.

At the same moment in time – March 2019 – across the Atlantic at Shakespeare's Globe, Lynette Linton and Adjua Andoh have co-directed *Richard II* in the Sam Wanamaker playhouse (Linton and Andoh, 2019), in the Globe's first ever all-women-of-colour production (see Section 4). Andoh, lately of *Bridgerton* fame and a long-time leading woman on UK stage and screen, plays Richard in a production jam-packed with cultural references to multiple parts of Africa, the Caribbean, and Asia. This is not some blanket attempt to locate the play in the Global South; it is a series of very specific choices designed to centre the women "at the bottom" of the empire's "heap" (in Andoh's words in the *Such Stuff* podcast, Shakespeare's Globe 2020). The cast are radiant in the ambient candlelight as it flickers across the bamboo screen that lines the back wall of the playing area; they can be at home all across this stage precisely because the work of designing for them, lighting and costuming their bodies, photographing, filming, and marketing their performances has been done by women of colour just like them. Later, I'll read interviews with Linton and Andoh and hear of the multiple challenges they faced to assemble their cast and crew and resource their needs properly; I'll also read about the incredible sense of ownership and belonging the cast were able to feel, over both space and story, once those needs were finally met. Right now, though, I am fixated by the photographs that line the playing space. Above the actors' heads, images of the cast and crew's grandmothers and other women ancestors look down, shining forth their strength and courage.

Now it's August 2022. I'm sitting masked in the Studio Theatre at the Stratford Festival (in Stratford, Ontario, Canada)[1] watching *1939* (2022) a new play co-written by Jani Lauzon (Métis) and Kaitlyn Riordan (see Section 2). The plot of *1939* takes place in a residential school, where young Indigenous children are housed by the Crown and the Catholic Church. The King and Queen of England are planning a visit to Canada, and the children of this school will put on a production of *All's Well That Ends Well* to showcase their skills. The performances are wonderful, but the story feels too gentle, at first, for the politically charged subject matter. (The violence perpetrated at residential schools in Canada was the subject of Canada's first Truth and Reconciliation Commission [2008–15].) I'm a frequent Stratford audience member and I'm used to seeing the Festival produce work that strives not to offend other frequent audience members, who are often older, white, and affluent. It feels to me like this is one of those shows. An hour later, however, I feel my inherent bias shift as I experience the play's climax. The student actors in *All's Well* become fed up with the "dime store Indian" production they are stuck in; they cast off their faux headdresses and perform a loud and joyous round dance in the middle of the Studio stage. Later, I'll learn that this production's is the first round dance ever performed at the Festival. Right now, though, as I leave the theatre I visit the community healing space that Lauzon and Riordan have set up to support audience members who want to talk about what they've witnessed. I observe quietly as a group of older spectators wearing orange Every Child Matters[2] T-shirts speak with an Elder about the harm they carry from their own residential school experiences.

This Element is an attempt to understand how and why artists like Dawn Jani Birley, Jani Lauzon, Adjua Andoh, and Lynette Linton choose to work with Shakespeare and his contemporaries – the early modern "classical" canon – at a moment in time when theatres around the world are striving toward equity, inclusion, diversity, and decolonization. I uplift women creators from equity-owed communities as I learn from them about how they transform plays we know to be patriarchy-affirming, ableist, and often racist into vehicles for community storytelling and models for radically inclusive and difference-centred ways of making. I use an ethnographic methodology (more on that a bit later in this section) as well as an intersectional feminist lens throughout, for all the women with whom I am in conversation necessarily make their art at the intersections of gender and ability, gender and race, gender and indigeneity,

---

[1] For further details about the Stratford Festival, including its history and its role in Canada's settler colonial present, see Section 2.

[2] More information about the Every Child Matters movement and Canada's Orange Shirt Day can be found here: https://nctr.ca/education/every-child-matters/.

and gender and the experience of transition. Ultimately, this Element is not about reading Shakespeare but about reading Shakespeare-in-process: the worlds I introduce us to are the worlds these creators build for themselves and their communities as they explore their complex relationships to Shakespeare in the creation room.

1.1 Investing in Shakespeare

Do you remember your first encounter with William Shakespeare? Did it feel like he was *for you*? I remember my first time; it was in junior high school. I was Mr F.'s star pupil in language arts class; on this day, whatever the lesson may have been, it ended with Mr F. invoking Shakespeare. We weren't studying any of the plays but I wanted to try reading them; I asked Mr F. for advice. He told me I should wait until I started high school. At the time I was ashamed; I thought he was telling me I wasn't smart enough to read Shakespeare by myself, that as a child of immigrants with no readers at home to guide me I wasn't ready for the great weight and power of The Bard. Now, in hindsight, I wonder if Mr F. was cannily deflecting. I wonder if Mr F. – an immigrants' kid like me – may have thought Shakespeare wasn't really for him, either.

Who "owns" Shakespeare? Who wants to own him, and why? Who is prepared to give up ownership to Shakespeare, and how do they even begin? What alternatives to "owning" Shakespeare might we discover if we turn away from our current industry model, in which Shakespeare operates as a form of global theatrical currency?

These are not rhetorical questions. Historically, the figure we call "Shakespeare" is an icon of colonial power, a figure whose works were used to advance the march of civilization across the British Empire in the eighteenth and nineteenth centuries. His plays and poems intentionally embed white supremacy (something I talk about in more detail in Section 4), and they have long been used to demarcate firm lines between "high" and "low" culture at the theatre, as well as to structure hierarchies based on social status and educational experience beyond the stage.[3] Today, Shakespeare continues to sit in pole position atop the sector we broadly label "the culture industries." For many

---

[3] Scholars have been examining Shakespeare's relationships to colonialism, to the development of post-colonial identities in former British colonies and settler colonial nations, and to racism and white supremacy for several decades. Path-breaking texts include Ania Loomba and Martin Orkin's (1998) *Post-Colonial Shakespeares* and Loomba's (2002) *Shakespeare, Race, and Colonialism*; Kim F. Hall's (1996) *Things of Darkness* and her special issue of *Shakespeare Quarterly* focused on early modern race studies, edited with Peter Erickson (Erickson and Hall 2016); Ayanna Thompson's (2011) *Passing Strange* and *The Cambridge Companion to Shakespeare and Race* (Thompson 2021); Arthur L. Little, Jr's (2022) *White People in Shakespeare*; and Farah Karim-Cooper's (2023) *The Great White Bard*.

theatre makers and lay theatre fans, he remains, foremost, a figure of elite, literary authority. As W. B. Worthen writes in *Shakespeare and the Authority of Performance*, "While the theatre is often described as licentious, promiscuous, innovative, imaginative, or merely haphazard in its representation of texts, to think of performance as conveying authorized meanings of any kind, especially meanings authenticated in and by the text, is, finally, to tame the unruly ways of the stage" (Worthen 1997, 3). In contradiction to the inherent instability (and democracy!) of playtexts cobbled from sides (actors' individual parts) and quartos edited by several hands into bound folios and eventually "complete works" over the course of the long early modern period, Worthen argues that both scholars and practitioners of elite Shakespeare (think the Royal Shakespeare Company [RSC]) use "the stage" as a place authorized to produce "authentically Shakespearean meanings" (3) – meanings from which both scholars and practitioners then borrow authority in turn, deploying their grasp of Shakespeare as powerful cultural capital to be spent elsewhere.

This marks the second key function today of the figure we call "Shakespeare": he is by now a global industry that promises access to significant social status and economic gain. "Shakespeare", as Why Not's Ravi Jain put it to me, "is Kleenex":[4] ubiquitous, familiar to everyone, useful to have around if you need a sell-out. "Shakespeare" is money in the bank. And this bankable ubiquity is one very good reason why so many people – people whom we might otherwise imagine would want nothing to do with colonialism's star export – are still interested in making and consuming Shakespeare's plays in the wake of #MeToo, Black Lives Matter, Land Back, and other decolonization movements. But it's also not the whole reason.

This is something I want to be clear about right up front: for the artists in this Element, Shakespeare is also a writer, an artist like them. At the end of the day, his legacy is also personal. These artists are women of colour; they are Black and Indigenous women; they are trans and non-binary women; and they are Deaf and blind women. They are committed anti-racists; they are disability justice advocates; they are advocates for trans rights. They fight every day for accessibility, inclusion, and decolonization – for them, that fight is personal. And they love Shakespeare; they choose him in this fight. Shakespeare's plays lie embedded in their early memories of reading together with family (Alex Bulmer; Emma Frankland; Yvette Nolan; Jani Lauzon) or working with an inspiring teacher at school (Dawn Jani Birley; Nataki Garrett). Shakespeare represents, for them, not the locked gate of high culture but rather an early

---

[4] M. Fernandes and R. Jain, personal interview, 7 December 2021.

experience of *access*. His words – alongside the cultural power they hold – are a part of how these women became the artists and leaders they are today.

But then, at some point (often more than one), every one of these women *also* received the message that Shakespeare *just wasn't for them*, after all. At drama school, in auditions, or in the persistent challenges they face when trying to make work on their own terms even now, at some point the gate to Shakespeare closed. These artists, as we'll see throughout this Element, make their work at the coalface, the exposed seam of contradictions that haunts us every time we try to account for the "authority" attached to Shakespeare. Their art and their fight benefit from recognizing both how it feels to claim a figure like Shakespeare – to love the verse with which "he" is synonymous; to see their own imagination and artistic potential refracted in his works – and also what it feels like to have access to those works and their accrued cultural authority taken away, as those with greater social, historical, and embodied privilege say, *It's not that you're not good, it's that you just don't fit the part.* These artists actively choose Shakespeare as a fellow traveler toward equity and social justice, but they combine their personal interests in everything "he" might be with a strong political awareness of how the very idea of Shakespeare has always been organized and gate-kept for the benefit of some and at the expense of others. Their love is necessarily dissonant, and their artistic processes – intersectional; cosmologically Indigenous; decentralized and non-hierarchical; committed to resource-sharing and mentorship – proudly foreground that dissonance as an equity-seeking move.

The question of just who or what "Shakespeare" is, what "his" authority means and can mean in the future, thus remains an open one – malleable, transformable, even transformational. As we meet these artists and explore their practices in the pages ahead, let's hold close the question of which Shakespeares they choose to activate, how, and for whose benefit.

1.2 Sustainable Investments

In a recent essay about Shakespeare and decolonization, Andrew Hartley, Kaja Dunn, and Christopher Berry ask, "Can [the history of Shakespeare as a tool for performing white cultural superiority] be circumvented or – better yet – rewritten, and what means might be attempted to accomplish this decolonizing process?" (Hartlet, Dunn, and Berry 2021, 171). My guiding question, "Who owns Shakespeare?", reframes this question to shine light on a paradox.[5]

---

[5] Excellent recent scholarship on Shakespeare and decolonization can be found in the pages of *Shakespeare Bulletin*, especially the Winter 2021 special issue on Shakespeare and social justice edited by David Sterling Brown and Sandra Young (2021). See also Kemp (2019) on trans

Shakespeare, especially when he is held up as a synonym for "great theatre" untouched by crass materialism, is always, first and foremost, about money, resources, and power. Our current economic climate is governed by neo-liberalism, a form of global financial capitalism that places ultimate faith in free markets to determine the distribution of resources and ultimate responsibility for economic failings on individuals. This framework primarily benefits those who already have significant resources; it values shareholder expectations over labour force needs and encourages individual wealth accumulation over community support and the equitable distribution of capital (Harvey 2005). Neo-liberalism's runaway success since the early 1980s has guaranteed that, no matter where you live, access to resources will be tied in some way to race, class, gender, and the other key status markers that determined how much you had to begin with.

In 2017, I published an essay called "Shakespeare's Property Ladder" (Solga 2017). In it I investigated how Britain's directorial landscape, as late as 2015, remained reluctant to allow all but the most "bankable" women artists the opportunity to direct major Shakespeare plays in mainstage venues. The inspiration for my title came from high-profile British director Katie Mitchell. In a 2011 National Theatre (NT) Platform discussion with Dan Rebellato, Mitchell explained why she has refused to direct Shakespeare across her substantial international career. She reflected on her one and only Shakespeare, *Henry VI: The Battle for the Throne* (at the RSC, 1994). She chose *Henry VI* specifically because it was obscure, less likely to provoke comparisons to past productions at the RSC, and thus less likely to draw the ire of the old guard at the RSC whom she knew regarded her youth, gender, and experimental practice with suspicion. She told Rebellato: "[There is a] deep sense of ownership of this material, maybe related to gender, owned maybe by men more than women (maybe)" (Mitchell and Rebellato 2011). This sense of ownership is exactly what Worthen would call, three years after Mitchell's *Henry*, the bulwarking of Shakespearean authority, and – as Mitchell might have predicted – RSC stakeholders excoriated her choices in *Battle for the Throne*, accusing her actors of sloppy verse speaking and her design concept of being contrary to Shakespeare's intentions. From that point on, her response to Shakespeare became: why bother?

Mitchell's declaration at the National still feels daring to me, however couched her language; it takes courage to tell the establishment to sod off and tenacity to go the distance on your own terms. But walking away from power is

---

dramaturgies in the early modern canon and Nora Williams (2022) on "incomplete" dramaturgies in the search for inclusive casting.

only possible when power and privilege are, on some level, yours already; as a white, cis-, Oxford-educated woman whose international star was in 1994 already rising, Mitchell lost comparatively little from turning her back on Shakespeare's currency. What of those without that level of existing privilege? What of those for whom the route isn't around Shakespeare but through?

The idea of ownership that I'm animating here has two valences. One is economic, to do with how resources are distributed in the staging of Shakespeare and whose interests that distribution serves. The other, however, is political, to do with both whom we think of when we think of his works – and also who *doesn't* come to mind. Shakespeare's political ownership is often tied to what are called the "universal" qualities of his characters and themes. But who comes to mind when we think of Shakespeare's verse? White, classically trained bodies, speaking in a very specific (British-accented) manner. Calling Shakespeare "universal" sounds inherently inclusive, a way of devolving access to everyone; several of the artists in the pages that follow would agree. But, as Ayanna Thompson reminds us, the very notion of "universal" Shakespeare has operated, historically, as a slick cover for the perpetuation of white colonial ownership. In her essential book about Shakespeare and race, *Passing Strange* (2011), Thompson writes that arguments about Shakespeare's timeless and placeless qualities have often been strategically connected to white supremacism via the practice of "colourblind casting," a version of tokenism that invites actors of colour to participate in productions of the plays only on the tacit condition that they not bring their own histories and experiences into the creation space with them (see also Catanese 2011). After all, if the production doesn't "see colour," and Shakespeare is already "for everyone," those stories can't be relevant, right? Thompson (2011, 38) notes that when we make this argument, "Shakespeare is taken to mean two contradictory, but not mutually exclusive, ideas: the exclusivity of Western civilization *and* the fantasy of the racial homogeneity of that civilization." In other words, Shakespeare's cultural capital – his economic power as a titan of today's culture industries, not to mention his legacy power as a civilizing emissary of the British Empire – derives directly from the assumption that his works and their authority "exclude everything that is not Western," but also that Western "civilization, culture, and society, which Shakespeare helped to create, have nothing to do with issues of race" (Thomson 2011, 38).

So how do we dismantle these deep-seated power structures, structures that let us pretend that doing Shakespeare is about skill and talent (rather than money, education, or inherited privilege) and that access to his work and its inherent acclaim is unfettered (rather than systemically racist, classist, and gendered)? In these pages I seek a wide range of possible answers in the testimony and examples of artists already engaged in the work of this dismantling, and from the fieldwork I was privileged to undertake I can offer three guiding principles for us to bear in mind.

First, we must confront the reality that Shakespeare has not been "for everyone," *ever*. Only when those historically excluded from the feeling that Shakespeare is "for them" are given a proper opportunity to lay claim to Shakespeare, to call Shakespeare "universal" on their own terms (see Knowles 2007, 63; Fowler and Solga in press), can we achieve equity. Importantly, "equity" here does not mean a generic equality of access to Shakespeare's works or Shakespearean stages; it means generating the scaffolds required to provide formerly marginalized artists and creators a fairness of footing so that they might even begin to imagine what access to Shakespeare and the "classical" canon could mean *on their own terms*. Equity in this sense is about resource, it is about democratizing notions of story, and it is about uplifting voices that have been too long silenced.

Thus my second guiding principle: the Shakespeare industry, having profited from it so fully, needs to make good on the idea of a "universal Shakespeare" by transferring money, material resources, rehearsal and creation space, and the power to hold that space safely, into the hands of historically excluded artists. Again, this does not just mean "giving space" to such artists; it means sharing without condition and supporting without insisting on control, using company models like those pioneered by Nataki Garrett at the Oregon Shakespeare Festival (OSF)[6] (Section 4) and by Why Not Theatre in Toronto (Section 3). Decolonization is not a metaphor but an active and intentional practice of returning land and resources taken without consent (Tuck and Yang 2012); making Shakespeare properly equitable therefore requires those of us with power and privilege to "share everything," as Why Not's motto states, "because more artists means more stories" (Why Not Theatre n.d.b). This resource return must prioritize hiring and mentoring strong leaders from equity-owed groups, and then supporting those leaders fully as they undertake their stated mandates so that they might build a ladder upward. Every one of the examples in this Element will demonstrate how important artistic leaders of different genders, abilities, and racial experiences are to uplifting the next generation of such leaders, making the move toward Shakespearean equity not just possible but sustainable.

Finally, we need to meet in story. Shakespeare's plays are all based on stories taken, magpie-like, from other sources, and this is story's power: it is communal, adaptable, accessible. Story is how we make ourselves and how we build our

---

[6] See the OSF's "Mission and Vision" at www.osfashland.org/company/mission-and-values.aspx [accessed 27 March 2023].

communities; it offers a way to reimagine our worlds. Playing "with words and story" is how we make things better for everyone,[7] how we "change the story for good" (Why Not Theatre n.d.a). Shakespeare's most significant power, for many of the artists in these pages, lies in his capacity to "play with words and story" and then inspire others to do likewise. Their Shakespeare isn't (just) a guru or a boss but also a fellow storyteller, another participant in a democratic devising process. As Adjua Andoh writes:

> I have a belief that when people have ownership of what they're engaged in, they commit to it. They're not doing it to please teacher. They're not doing it because they're scared, they're doing it *because it's theirs*. . . . the variety of people who came [to *Richard II*] with something deep and precious and it's like everybody put it in your bank account. And they said, 'Here's my investment', and then when we did the play, we drew on all our investments to make it work. (Andoh 2021, 23)

1.3 Changing How We Tell the Story; Changing Whose Stories We Tell

My goal in this Element is to amplify the voices of women-identified creators who are actively making Shakespeare differently, in line with the principles I outline in Section 1.2. I strive to relate the fundamentals of their creative practices, the social ethos and the political goals behind those practices, and wherever possible I let these creators speak in their own words. This Element is not, therefore, about representations of Shakespeare's plays that look or sound or feel different, more inclusive, decolonized; it's about what happens long before the stage lights come up on those productions.

In order to centre artists in this way I use an ethnographic approach, drawing primarily from interviews I conducted for this research in collaboration with my research associate Dr Sheetala Bhat, as well as from interviews with artists and their collaborators broadcast or published elsewhere.[8] As a scholar trained in the reading and theorizing of literary and theatrical texts, I have had to learn a significant number of new things, both practical and ethical, in order to undertake this work in a wise way. My learning has also been, to some extent, an unlearning, a necessary recalibration of the unspoken centres and margins of scholarly work. How often have literary scholars, for example, been told that an author's intentions do not matter to the meanings of their writing? How many of us who work in theatre programmes know all too well the entrenched divisions

---

[7] R. Arluk, personal interview, 21 January 2022.

[8] Full ethics approval for this research has been obtained from Western University's Non-Medical Research Ethics Board. All interviewees provided informed consent, either written or verbal, for the sharing of materials from their interviews included here.

and the subtle hierarchies that divide the "scholars" from the "practitioners" on faculty? How many of us have been trained to mistrust the convictions of the artists whose work we read or hear or see, to treat those convictions as either naïve or irrelevant to critique?

Writing "Shakespeare's Property Ladder" (Solga 2017) convinced me that the stories I wanted to tell about Shakespeare were increasingly not on the stage but behind and before it – stories about access, resource, power, and account-ability. This in turn meant that my approach to talking about making Shakespeare had to change. In 2018, my colleague Dr Erin Julian and I shadowed Chinese-Canadian actor and director Keira Loughran as she strove to build a non-binary production of *The Comedy of Errors* at Ontario's Stratford Festival. We chronicled our journey in a 2021 article about Loughran's struggle to practise diversity thoroughgoingly at Stratford (Julian and Solga 2021). After composing our first draft we shared the article with Loughran, who offered frank and firm feedback that challenged many of our initial conclusions. That process of interlocution was difficult. It required us to recognize that Loughran's intentions *did* matter to what we made of the resulting show; they required us to reconsider our criticisms of the process and the eventual produc-tion while holding her point of view clearly in mind alongside our own. This did not, I will stress, require us to change what we saw as some of the most fundamental problems the production faced, but it did require that we assess those problems multidimensionally and with compassion, while understanding that we were not the only stakeholders whose version of events mattered. Having a challenging dialogue about the fundamentals of collaborative practice, and about our points of disagreement over its core tenets, allowed all three of us to deepen our understanding of the issues at stake and to recalibrate how to communicate them effectively (see also Loughran in press).

This Element, like that essay, strives for both nuance and generosity. Its primary mode is relational, and it shares practitioners' stories to make some claims about what is needed, both materially and politically, so that Shakespeare can become sustainably equitable, even possibly, someday, decolonial. I begin in Section 2 with Indigenous artists from Turtle Island: Jani Lauzon (Métis), Yvette Nolan (Algonquin, Irish), and Reneltta Arluk (Inuvialuk, Denesuline, Gwich'in, and Cree) and their entanglements with *All's Well That Ends Well*, *Julius Caesar*, and *MacBeth*, respectively. In Section 3 I focus on intersections, exploring the making of *Prince Hamlet* with Deaf creator Dawn Jani Birley, the making of *R&J* (an adaptation of *Romeo and Juliet* [Shakespeare 1597/1599]) with blind actor and voice coach Alex Bulmer, and the making of *Galatea* (a play by Shakespeare influencer John Lyly) with transwoman and force of nature Emma Frankland. In Section 4, I turn to two institutions helmed by women at this change point: Shakespeare's Globe (Michelle Terry, artistic director) and the Oregon Shakespeare Festival (OSF) (Nataki Garrett, artistic director 2019–23). In Sections 2 and 3, I explore the utopic power of decentred, community-focused creation spaces, paying attention to the role that practice-as-research (PaR) can play in advancing our understanding of a much queerer and less conventionally conservative Shakespearean universe. Later, in Sections 3, 4, and 5, I turn to issues of money and resource, exploring models that work, and models that falter, in uplifting the next generation of early modern makers.

2 Indigenous Creators

In this section I spotlight three Indigenous women from Turtle Island who make Shakespeare work for their communities. They cannily leverage their relationships with major Canadian arts institutions, their status as artistic Elders, and the plays' own tools to build community skill and capacity, foster growth and potential, and strengthen ties among Indigenous youth, Elders, and those in between. These artists are women of the "middle" generation:[9] they each have parent(s) who survived residential school,[10] and they were educated in a later twentieth-century colonial system that prioritized Shakespeare and other Anglo-European traditions and featured minimal, if any, learning about colonization and Indigeneity. Jani Lauzon (Métis), Yvette Nolan (Algonquin and Irish), and Reneltta Arluk (Inuvialuk, Denesuline, Gwich'in, and Cree) all claim Shakespeare proudly as part of their blended heritage; they see deep value in and feel strong love for the plays, and they recognize and treat Shakespeare "as a decolonizing force"[11] in the long game of restitution and reconciliation. For those of us trained to understand Shakespeare as a bad colonial hangover, this may come as a surprise.

In *Decolonizing Methodologies* (Tuhiwai Smith [1999] 2021), Linda Tuhiwai Smith (Ngāti Awa, Ngāti Porou, Tūhourangi) presents a wide range of strategies to help settler students and academics (of which I'm one[12]) recognize the colonial roots of what counts as knowledge and who counts as

---

[9] R. Arluk, personal interview, 21 January 2022.
[10] Residential schools in Canada operated from 1851 through the 1990s, supported by the Catholic Church as well as the British and then the Canadian federal governments. Their mandate was cultural genocide: they separated children from their families and banned the speaking of Indigenous languages. Physical and sexual violence was common, and many children who died while in residential school were buried in unmarked graves that are only now being excavated. Extensive information about the history of the residential school system and the findings and calls to action of the Truth and Reconciliation Commission (2008–15) are archived at https://nctr.ca/education/teaching-resources/residential-school-history/.
[11] R. Arluk, personal interview, 21 January 2022.
[12] I grew up in Treaty 6 territory in what is also called Edmonton, Alberta, Canada. (Treaty 6 was originally signed in August and September 1876 between members of the Cree and Stoney

its keepers. She encourages us to think carefully about whose version of reality much academic research supports, and to reflect on how the academic hierarchy between presumed "experts" and their research "subjects" prevents equitable knowledge sharing between Indigenous and non-Indigenous communities. Tuhiwai Smith also recognizes that the work of decolonizing praxis – be it academic or artistic – requires an at-times awkward balance: "Knowledge *and the power to define what counts as real knowledge* lie at the epistemic core of colonialism. The challenge for researchers … is to simultaneously work with colonial and Indigenous concepts of knowledge, decentring one while centring the other" (Tuhiwai Smith [1999] 2021, xii, my emphasis).

Lauzon, Nolan, and Arluk all work in the fine balance between the Indigenous cosmologies that shape their families, histories, and communities; the Western theatrical practices that have organized their education, training, and professional experiences as makers; and the economic realities of operating within an Indigenous theatre ecology that is still dependent on colonial models of capitalism. Their Shakespeares emerge from their "simultaneous working with" alongside their active re-centring of an ontologically different, more reciprocal method of creation.

2.1 Learning to Talk in Circles

The Stratford Festival in Stratford, Ontario, is not the kind of place where you expect to find a sacred fire burning on the front lawn.[13] Stratford's Shakespeare festival was established in the early 1950s to bring "the best" of British theatre to Canadian soil in what its founders broadly construed as a civilizing mission couched in a new nationalist language.[14] While long-needed change is now finally underway at Stratford, the festival's colonial roots are systemically entrenched, making any process of decolonization a huge structural challenge. Stratford works on a repertory model: both cast and crew work in "tracks" on two or three shows a season, and their labour as well as their time are scheduled accordingly. Casts are announced months in advance, and by the time the actors arrive at rehearsal the set and costume designs are largely fixed and the

---

nations and the British Crown.) I now live and work on land governed by the Between the Lakes Purchase (1792), the London Township and Sombra Treaties (1796), and the Dish With One Spoon Wampum Belt Covenant, in what is also called Southwestern Ontario. These lands are the traditional territories of the nêhiyaw, Dene, Anishinaabe, Nakota Isga, Niitsitapi, and a Métis homeland; and of the Erie, Neutral, Huron-Wendat, Haudenosaunee, Anishinaabe, Lūnaapéewak, and Chonnonton peoples.

[13] For Indigenous peoples, fire is a gift from the Creator, and sacred fires are used as part of Indigenous ceremonies to open doors to the spirit world and to communicate with ancestors. Sacred fire is considered central to wellness and healing in many Indigenous traditions.

[14] A number of Canadian scholars of Shakespeare have written extensively about Stratford's colonial heritage. See Knowles 1995 and 2004; Parolin 2009; Julian and Solga 2021.

directors' visions are firmly in place. Under these conditions, holistic collaboration across a creative team becomes very hard.

Jani Lauzon refers to Stratford as a series of theatrical "silos."[15] Many theatres built on the European model forged in the long nineteenth century work this way, and this way of working reflects and reproduces those theatres' colonial-era entanglements. Lauzon explicitly links the "silo" model and the land grant system that carved up and parcelled out the Canadian prairie to settlers in the nineteenth century: "just like the whole basis of colonial thinking, [it's] here's my little square, and here's my little square," she says.[16] While many Turtle Island first nations traditionally treated the land as a communal source of sustenance, when the British colonial government pursued its settler-based system of Indigenous genocide in the nineteenth century it drew square borders to make parcels of arable land and installed settler farmers on individual patches. The square then suffocated those who had farmed in circles: "you put a square over top of a circle and suddenly somebody [for example, Indigenous communities forced onto reservations] ends up with a piece of land where it's Canadian shield and you can't grow a thing and they starve."[17]

Jani Lauzon is an Elder in the Indigenous theatre communities of northern Turtle Island. Lauzon's father (Métis) was an artist and her mother (Scandinavian, whom she lost at twelve) was interested in spiritualism and the occult; she was raised by a foster family that included a high-school drama teacher with a deep, inspiring love of Shakespeare. She subsequently trained in a rich, eclectic mix of Japanese ritual and Indigenous spiritual practices (with Yoshi Oïda and Floyd Favel), alongside traditional Western theatre models including Shakespeare (which she calls "her thing") (Lauzon 2016). Her contemporary practice is multimedial – she is an award-winning musician, a puppeteer, a director, a stage and screen actor, and a playwright – and her influence is extensive. During the Covid-19 pandemic, she was appointed one of more than a dozen members of Stratford's anti-racism committee; the committee heard testimony from all corners of the Festival and issued a report packed with guidance on ways to adjust and begin to dismantle the structures that normalize racist aggression, keep artists sequestered from one another, and keep young creators working in fear of reporting aggressions that might impact their future at the Festival or beyond.[18] One of the most important

---

[15] J. Lauzon, personal interview with Hanna Shore, 14 August 2022.

[16] J. Lauzon, personal interview with Hanna Shore, 14 August 2022.

[17] J. Lauzon, personal interview with Hanna Shore, 14 August 2022.

[18] J. Lauzon, personal interview with Hanna Shore, 14 August 2022. Full details about the Stratford Festival's equity, diversity, and inclusion investigatory process, and the report of the anti-racism committee, can be accessed here: www.stratfordfestival.ca/landingpages/anti-racism.

recommendations to arise from the report was how to make the first day of rehearsals at the Festival better for everyone involved.

That's why Lauzon and Kaitlyn Riordan, her *1939* co-playwright, built that fire outside their rehearsal building and convened a conversation around it in summer 2022. During a panel talk that September, facilitated by their research dramaturg Sorouja Moll (mixed-race, settler), Riordan – who is a co-founder of and long-time director with feminist and social justice-oriented theatre company Shakespeare in the Ruff (Toronto), where Lauzon has played Paulina in *A Winter's Tale* and Shylock in *The Merchant of Venice* – described the surprise the fire brought to their Stratford peers: "everyone else at Stratford was like, 'you had a fire?? What?? We want to have a fire! We just talked about how to put on our wigs" (Lauzon, Moll, and Riordan 2022). Instead of starting with wigs or a tour of the design maquette, Lauzon and Riordan invited Elders Liz Stevens (Anishinaabe) and Phil Davis (Haundenosaunee) to lead both cast and crew: "Instead of talking about the play we just talked about ourselves, and we talked about each other, and we smudged together, and we sat around a sacred fire together, and we just got to know each other" (Lauzon, Moll, and Riordan 2022). For Lauzon, this work of gathering in a circle and sharing our most grounding stories is the first step in the reconciliation process in settler spaces like Stratford, and also the first step in creating a good play together. Only after this sharing process concluded did Lauzon place their script – including parts of Shakespeare's *All's Well* – in the middle of the circle, where it could join the stories already offered there.

2.2 Who Discovered Who?

The play *1939* was conceived when Lauzon and Riordan met for coffee to talk about the possibility of Lauzon directing for Shakespeare in the Ruff; the gig didn't work out, but after the two spent ages "geeking out" over their shared love of Shakespeare, they determined to write a play together (Lauzon, Moll, and Riordan 2022). Five years of extensive research and workshops later, *1939* received its world premiere at Stratford's Studio Theatre in August 2022. Set in a residential school modelled on the Shingwauk school in Sault Ste-Marie, Ontario in the year in which King George VI made his first royal visit to Canada, the play follows five students – brother and sister Joseph (Richard Comeau) and Beth (Tara Sky, who is Lauzon's daughter), Susan (Kathleen MacLean), Evelyne (Wahsonti:io Kirby), and Jean (John Wamsley) – who are chosen to perform *All's Well That Ends Well* for the Crown. Their teacher Sian Ap Dafydd (Sarah Dodd) is a Welsh woman who has internalized her own experience of British colonial oppression and insists on forced English accents and pronunci-ation à la Ellen Terry; the students, however, develop other ideas as they begin to work with the play in the rhythms of their own languages and ancestral teachings.

From this cursory description, *1939* sounds like a feel-good show in which some underdog kids prove their teachers wrong as they discover themselves through Shakespeare. "Discover yourself" in the play is a typical request made by white directors of Shakespeare to actors of all kinds; Brandi Wilkins Catanese (2011) relates exactly such an experience in her book *The Problem of the Color[blind]*. Playing Rosalind from *As You Like It* for a scene study in college, she had to swear by her "white hand"; she stumbled repeatedly trying to make sense of the line for herself and her Black skin. Finally, she chose to make the "mistake" of her mismatched hand funny: laughter seemed the easiest, least painful way out for performer and spectator alike. "I didn't quite know what to do," she writes, "so I took it as my responsibility to demonstrate my awareness of my nonnormative performing body, and to diminish its significance by laughing it off. I was, as David Wiles puts it, 'trying to live in the "world of the play" while performing in the world of race'" (Catanese 2011, 10).

In *1939*, this demand to erase the world of race (and Indigeneity) in service to the world of the play is confronted – and reversed. Beth, Joe, Susan, Evelyne, and Jean are unaware that they are not supposed to access Helena's and Bertram's stories on their own terms. When they are left by the exasperated Mrs Ap Dafydd to figure out how to improve their struggling speeches – to solve, like Brandi Catanese, the problem *of themselves* – they decide to do some practice-based research. In a pivotal scene, the students work together to map out an Indigenous community from the basics of the play's plot and characters; it features a range of national identities, to account for the mix of Anishinaabe (Ojibway), Haundenosaunee (Mohawk), and Métis (mixed Indigenous and French) identities in their cohort. They plot this new community on a blackboard, adjusting and readjusting with input from everyone. As they talk and draw, they uncover important parallels between the play's stories and their own lived experiences. Evelyne, who plays Helena, makes a profound discovery: Helena is an orphan, like her, whose father was a healer, like Evelyne's grandfather, and now she alone holds the power to cure the King of France. Evelyne concludes that Helena has medicine, passed down through generations, and even though she has been lost to her own community, the medicine's power remains with her. She declares, bold and overjoyed: "Helena is a Mohawk girl, like me!" Mrs Ap Daffyd is, predictably, appalled. Like Catanese, whose work on Rosalind was meant to be the work of Black erasure, Evelyne is supposed to work out how to erase the Indian in her performance of Helena. Instead, Evelyne *uncovers the Haudenosaunee in Helena*, the (literal) ground where their stories can meet.

"What makes ideas 'real' is the system of knowledge, the formations of culture, and the relations of power in which these concepts are located," writes Tuhiwai Smith ([1999] 2021, 55). The European imperial project overwrote Indigenous land with borders and deeds of ownership (squares dropped onto circles), just as it overwrote Indigenous origin stories and ancestral knowledge-keeping practices with a logocentric, hierarchical framing co-authored by Christianity and white supremacy and cemented in "official" history books and in the dissemination of white cultural texts like Shakespeare's (Tuhiwai Smith [1999] 2021, 36–8). Different stories can be told; we just haven't yet learned that they, too, are "real." In fact, the kind of PaR that Evelyne and her peers undertake in their creation process is increasingly used today by blended teams of early modern artists and scholars to help tease out the stories of gender non-conformity, ability difference, and pervasive non-whiteness that is rife in the early modern canon. In action, PaR is an "iterative" (Davies in press) and process-oriented methodology that brings diverse artist and scholar bodies and their lived histories into dialogue with historical texts; it asks questions about what new realities emerge when history lands in our mouths, arms, feet, or when props animate historical assumptions in the space between two performing bodies.[19] As Peter Cockett and Melinda Gough remind us, early modern theatre history is "built on fragments" of evidence from a period in which "the power of cis-patriarchy" and its colonizing projects "could be violently enforced" (Cockett and Gough in press, introduction). When we bring fragments of the past into dialogue with present imagination, we reanimate stories hidden by design. In this way, PaR promises to uplift and render "real" the repertoires of knowledge suppressed by the textocentrism of colonial practice.

It was a healer from Manitoulin Island who first helped Lauzon see the connection between Helena and Evelyne, convincing her that *All's Well* was the right play to place within *1939*. And it was an Elder from Six Nations (a large Haudenosaunee community situated along the Grand River outside Toronto) whom Lauzon met at an Indigenous-led performance of *The Tempest* in the 1990s who told her, "when you are Indigenous and you do Shakespeare you need to be super careful" because "the energy around Shakespeare's plays is so large and so spiritual that you don't want to mess with it" (Lauzon, Moll, and Riordan 2022). For Lauzon, this teaching was life- and practice-changing. It did not ask her to revere Shakespeare as an artistic or spiritual superior; it asked her to understand each of his plays as the holder of an embodied spirit, and the making

---

[19] The multinational Engendering the Stage project is a formidable example of the power of PaR to re-story early modern theatre's gendered histories; see Cockett and Gough in press. See also Section 3, in which I discuss the PaR process that resulted in Frankland's *Galatea*. For more on the queerness of the English stage "before" Shakespeare, see https://beforeshakespeare.com.

of a play in performance as an act of ceremony in which each member of a creative team is equally responsible to the play, to their own stories, to their ancestors, and to each other.

From this and other Elder teachings (including from Pauline Shirt [Cree], Justine Enosse and Edna Manitowabi [both Wikwemikong First Nation, Manitoulin Island]), Lauzon's "circular" rehearsal room dramaturgy emerged.[20] The play goes "in the centre," and all labour in the room is devoted to "feeding the spirit of the play" (Lauzon, Moll, and Riordan 2022). This model of working in the round derives from a cosmology that prioritizes reciprocity and accountability to the spirit world, the land, and to one another, and that understands artistry as integral to all aspects of living, including the work of the law, practices of daily life, governance relations, and more (Lauzon 2016, 92). Lauzon's "centring" of the play thus ironically enacts an important cosmo-logical shift away from colonial ways of working (in which Shakespeare goes in the centre), and toward an understanding of the play *as shared story*, to which we all have access and to which we all have a shared responsibility that is both spiritual and artistic, as well as part of the art of surviving everyday life.

2.3 No More Hungry Listening

In the spirit of PaR, Lauzon's research practice mirrors her circular dramaturgy in its ability to hold many stories and realities in view at once. The *1939* research team included those from traditional research backgrounds, like Sorouja Moll, who offered "academic knowledge and access to documentation" about the history of Shakespeare in colonial Canada, as well as an "oral research team" of Elders including Pauline Shirt, Shirley Horn (Cree and a survivor of the Shingwauk school), and Liz Stevens (Anishinaabe) who provided "research through lived experience" (Lauzon, Moll, and Riordan 2022). Tuhiwai Smith explains that "research" is a "dirty word" for many Indigenous communities because they have long been "subjects" (or indeed objects) of academic research that has sought to extract knowledge from them without reciprocity or respect for ontological differences (Tuhiwai Smith [1999] 2021, 1). Stōlo musicologist Dylan Robinson calls this form of colonial knowledge extraction "hungry listening." The hungry settler-listener,[21] in Robinson's framing, is a kind of Windigo, the insatiable cannibal spirit that crosses several different

---

[20] J. Lauzon, personal interview with Hanna Shore, 14 August 2022.
[21] Robinson defines "settler" as a "positionality" rather than a fixed identity category, "a stratified and intersectional process, a particular normative structure of experience, feeling and the sensible" (Robinson 2020, 95). As Lauzon, Moll, and Riordan (2022) note, there's an important difference on Turtle Island between "settler" ancestors of long-present European populations and newcomer settlers, which in Canada include, for example, numerous refugee populations.

Indigenous cosmologies. Hungry settler-listeners, then as now, consume Indigenous artistry looking for any number of extractable morsels: aesthetic pleasure; a frisson of the exotic; stories of trauma and healing; a path toward reconciliation; the erasure of settler guilt (Robinson 2020, 106). This extraction is one-sided: the auditor understands themself as a consumer and imagines the art is "for them." This extractive mentality comes at a severe cost.

Robinson explains that, while much Western music is primarily aesthetic, Indigenous music is both "aesthetic" and "functional" (Robinson 2020, 95): "This is to say [Indigenous songs] are history, teaching, law that takes the form of song, just as western forms of law and history take the form of writing" (Robinson 2020, 100). Indigenous sonic practice is world-making through sound, just as Anglo-European written histories, for example, are world-making through text. Indigenous sonic practice, importantly, also includes "listening as a component in the act of making something happen, of bringing something into being" (Robinson 2020, 100) – the auditor not as cannibal or thief but as fellow storyteller, as participant.

The lived experience of *1939*'s oral research team included experience with languages, and with the knotty problem that, for many Indigenous residents of Turtle Island (including many in the cast and crew), ancestral languages and the knowledge contained in their soundings have been lost. During the play's rehearsal period, Elder researcher Liz Stevens' experience as an Anishinaabek speaker led to discussions with Riordan and Lauzon about what language means for Indigenous communities. "Language is culture," Stevens noted, echoing Robinson; "A language holds its culture within it, its values, its point of view in the world" (Lauzon, Moll, and Riordan 2022). This teaching in turn led the creative team, in collaboration with Wahsonti:io Kirby (the actor playing Helena), to translate pieces of text, including Helena's pivotal "Our remedies oft in ourselves do lie" speech, into Kanyen'kéha, in which Kirby is fluent. Part of the team's realization in the translation process was that the speech could not directly be converted; the culture, values, and point of view were distant enough to make literal translation from the play's verse into Kanyen'kéha meaningless. Instead, the words passed from seventeenth-century Shakespearean English into twenty-first century Canadian English and then into twenty-first century Mohawk, modulated by speakers of Anishinaabemowin, Kanyen'kéha, and English. Kirby was then able to articulate Helena's experience refracted through the kaleidoscopic cultures, histories, and points of view of two young Indigenous women (her own self and this play's Helena) based not in fictional seventeenth-century France or in Shakespeare's England but on Turtle Island in 2022.

Indigenous sounding takes over near the end of *1939*, when the students' show finally goes up. Beth, Joe, Susan, Evelyne, and Jean may have successfully imagined an Indigenous world for their *All's Well*, but it gets taken over by the colonial thrust of their teachers and by local settler women (in an ironic nod to theatrical silos?) who costume them in "beads and buckskin" without consultation (Nolan 2014, 228). Lauzon is interested in realities that are generally invisible, though, and thus audiences to *1939* see the performance from backstage: we watch as the frustrated student actors skitter back and forth in Pocahontas-style outfits carrying ridiculous prop canoes, and we hear music-hall sounds blended with canned audience laughter to reinforce the goofiness. At the interval, the student performers are exhausted, well and truly fed up with this painful mockery of their story. They look at each other; then, one by one, they pull off their faux head-dresses. They form a circle, lift their voices into the air, and perform a resounding round dance in the middle of the Stratford Studio stage (see Figure 1).

This was the first time in the Festival's history that a round dance had been performed at Stratford – but, as Lauzon notes, without any doubt round dances would have been held on the lands Stratford now occupies for centuries before European arrival. The students' round dance re-sounds the ancestors who would have danced on the land beneath the building beneath their feet, echoing the contemporary round dances associated with the Idle No More and Land Back protest movements across Turtle Island. Sitting stage left of the Studio's thrust,

Figure 1 From left: Richard Comeau as Joseph Summers, John Wamsley as Jean Delorme, Kathleen MacLean as Susan Blackbird, Wahsonti:io Kirby as Evelyne Rice, and Tara Sky as Beth Summers in *1939* (Stratford Festival, 2022). Photography by David Hou.

I felt the dance in my body, reverberating through the floor. The sound blanketed us all, energizing our shared space, our collective bodies. It was the co-creation of a historic moment: a call to witness, and a demand for reciprocity in the re-sounding of a seemingly familiar story.

2.4 "Tee-Hee, Brutus!"

Yvette Nolan knows all about settler resistance to hearing Shakespeare's stories differently. In 2008, she and an all-Indigenous creative team opened *Death of a Chief*, their adaptation of *Julius Caesar*, at the National Arts Centre (NAC) in Ottawa; the NAC acted as a co-producer of the work alongside Toronto-based Native Earth Performing Arts (NEPA), which Nolan led as artistic director from 2003 until 2011. The reviews were practically caricatures of the hungry listening Robinson (2020) describes, and Nolan has written eloquently back to them. Reviewers (including two white cis- men from two leading national newspapers, as well as an Asian woman) wanted the show to explain to them the symbolism of its set design (the central circle was a medicine wheel), what *Julius Caesar* could possibly have to do with contemporary "Native" concerns, and they really (really) wanted the actors to sound more "Indian" (they wanted "rez speak," as Nolan puts it) (Nolan 2014, 226). The show did not offer them the kind of "Native" they expected, and they certainly never expected Indigenous voices lifted in Shakespeare's verse. They didn't hear what they wanted to hear, and they didn't even try to understand what they *were* hearing. Despite this "critical" reception, *Death of a Chief* played to near-capacity audiences at the NAC, and Nolan and her team received plenty of anecdotal feedback that what they were sharing was deeply wanted by both settler and Indigenous audiences.[22] This was, in many ways, a show made for a community hearing. It was, in fact, a show made *in order to build a community* – in exactly the way Indigenous art practices are literally performative and "do" things like enact laws or treaties (Robinson 2020). *Death of a Chief* was not just about making a play; like *1939*, it used Shakespeare's language and story as tools of community creation, in the service of building a shared path to Indigenous artistic survivance.

When my research assistant Sheetala Bhat and I met with Nolan on Zoom in December 2021, she was eager to tell us the story of how she first met Shakespeare. She's told this story before (to Sorouja Moll 2006), but like any good Elder she loves to retell it. Like Lauzon, whose foster father was a high-school drama teacher, Nolan benefited from parents with literary foundations. Her mother was a residential school survivor who (like the students of *1939*) wasn't aware of what she *wasn't* supposed to learn; she borrowed volume after

---

encyclopedia volume from the library, developing a lifelong love of wordplay. Nolan remembers sitting down, about age three, with her mom and *Julius Caesar* on TV. When her father came home from work and asked about the day, Yvette declared gleefully that when Caesar died he said, "Tee hee, Brutus!"[23]

Playing in and with Shakespeare's plays, and especially his words, has been central to Nolan's lifelong practice as an artist. There's nothing "precious" about Shakespeare, for her, and "if it's not precious it can be playful."[24] Trained in literary criticism, Nolan was never told at the University of Manitoba that Shakespeare was off-limits, and she excelled at studying the plays. In Winnipeg, working with the Theatre Alliance, she made short pieces as part of a series designed as a "testing ground," including a four person *Othello* with Black and Indigenous actors that was cross-gendered. At just twenty minutes long, this was Shakespeare "boiled down to the story."[25] Arriving in 2003 at NEPA, Canada's oldest Indigenous theatre company, Nolan soon had actors coming to her to tell her they could not get auditions for Shakespeare, and, if by chance they did, they did not know how to "get the gig." Nolan asked Kennedy C. McKinnon, a voice coach at Stratford, to do a Shakespeare intensive for all interested NEPA artists; after the workshop they returned to Nolan and said: "Okay, so now we need a production to use the tools!" *Death of a Chief* began from a clear and basic community need – the need for theatrical tools to get good, higher-profile jobs for working Indigenous theatre artists – and it was always designed to be a place where a group of actors who had been gate-kept away from Shakespeare in their childhoods, training, or careers could build new skills. The process of moving the show from intensive, through workshops, and finally into production took three years; along the way it became a framework for "developing the community" that was growing up around it.[26]

Nolan didn't just choose *Julius Caesar* because it was familiar to her from her childhood; the choice was political. *Caesar* is a story about leadership structures, about what happens to a community when it grows disillusioned with its leaders, and about how better models of governance can emerge from the "tearing down" of leaders no longer fit for purpose.[27] The growing *Chief* community talked together about First Nations Band politics, the challenges of leading those historically oppressed into effective self-determination, and the importance of reckoning with the colonial imposition of patriarchy across many First Nations communities (Moll 2006). Nolan – who at the time of our

---

[23] Y. Nolan, personal interview, 15 December 2021.

[24] Y. Nolan, personal interview, 15 December 2021.

[25] Y. Nolan, personal interview, 15 December 2021.

[26] Y. Nolan, personal interview, 15 December 2021.

[27] Y. Nolan, personal interview, 15 December 2021.

interview was pursuing a master's degree in public policy at the University of Saskatchewan – saw in *Caesar* another kind of tool: a rehearsal for more equitable Indigenous self-government. Of the *Chief* process she writes:

> Over the next three years, we held workshops, working with the text, choosing what spoke to us, exploding the timelines and putting the scenes back together, often simultaneously. More importantly, perhaps, we negotiated over the years our own kind of self-government within the company. We were, after all, a company drawn from a host of nations: Mohawk, Guna, Rappahannock, Wampanoag, Métis, Gwich'in, Algonquin, Cree, Ojibwe, Tuscarora. We each brought our own teachings and traditions to the room – in some cultures women do not drum, some are matrilineal – and negotiated a new set of rules for this community, this Rome, Ontario. We self-governed. And that which we did in the room, we extended into the play, and in my heart I could imagine a way forward for First Nations in Canada. (Nolan 2014, 224)

While not all members of the *Death of a Chief* community came from matrilineal nations, the initial shaping of that community was fully matrilineal. The process began with Nolan, alongside Kennedy McKinnon and Michelle St John, convening workshops for all interested cast members. The women (it was all women) who had taken the initial intensive came consistently; men also came, but not all were invited to return. ("If they were not willing to learn to play the way we were playing . . . according to the values [of] generosity and humility and courage," then, Nolan exclaims with characteristic glee, "we would be, 'okay, these guys are out!'"[28] (see also Knowles 2007, 57). Nolan describes the resulting room as a collaborative space of peer teaching, with members of the cast who had done significant amounts of Shakespeare (like Lauzon, who played Marc Anthony, and Monique Mojica, who played Caesar) supporting and coaching those new to the tools.[29] She also points out that since she, too, had no formal theatre training, let alone training in directing Shakespeare, authority over form, content, and technique was shared across the room. Discussion, while not always easy, could make space for what everyone had brought with them into the room, as well as what was missing.

Of course, even a room with a novice director can be less than equitable; what made the *Death of a Chief* room different was the same circular economy that I described earlier in relation to Jani Lauzon's dramaturgy. (As a member of the *Chief* community, Lauzon was no doubt learning throughout that process as well.) This room ran as all other NEPA rehearsal rooms did during and after Nolan's tenure as artistic director: as a circle, not a triangle, and according to the Seven Grandfather Teachings (wisdom, love, respect, bravery, honesty,

---

[28] Y. Nolan, personal interview, 15 December 2021.
[29] Y. Nolan, personal interview, 15 December 2021.

humility, and truth; Manitowabi 2018). Lauzon's circle is based on the divestiture of ego: if the play in the centre has a spirit, and the spirit is our collective responsibility, we must place its and one another's needs before our own, secure in the knowledge that our needs will be held in the same way by all others undertaking the work with us. Nolan's circle, similarly, is based on a principle of shared investment in community because the making of the play is conceived as literally the work of building a new community, based on Indigenous creation principles negotiated in the room together. Along the way, the story of the play helps give that community shape, coordinates, and a direction in which to negotiate shared values. Nolan describes a moment later in the process when the fundamentals of the *Caesar* story became an obstacle for the community in this self-actualizing process:

> [T]he company stopped, and they're like, okay we need to know what we want for this community. Why do we keep getting rid of these leaders? What if we could have a Rome, Ontario that we wanted, what would it look like? And we just stopped and put up paper [on the wall] and wrote those lists: these are the values of the community. These are the things we aspire to. And I went, [exhales], OKAY, let's go forward! And we went forward, because now we knew what we'd lost – which is something that's articulated in the text, what's been lost and what's been stolen – and we knew what we wanted to get back to.[30]

All of this is what *Death of a Chief*'s reviewers chose not to hear as they listened for a "Native" Shakespeare. The *Toronto Star* reviewer[31] wrote that he could imagine *some* plays done this way – he singled out *A Midsummer Night's Dream* ("because apparently fairies can be Aboriginal") and *Coriolanus* ("because he struggles to adapt to a consensus-based community") – but not *Caesar* (Nolan 2014, 223). As Nolan notes, this "pronouncement raises a number of questions about how Indigenous creators are mediated, and by whom, and how the arbiter shapes the idea of Indigenous" (Nolan 2014, 223), echoing both Tuhawai Smith's comments on colonial research frameworks and Robinson's theorization of extractivist settler listening practices. Later in the same essay, Nolan recalls learning about Shakespeare's Globe's search for "a Native Canadian Shakespeare" for the Globe2Globe festival that ran in conjunction with London's Cultural Olympiad in 2012. She emailed festival producer Tom Bird with the suggestion of *Chief*. "He asked me what language the production was in," because Globe2Globe's hook was thirty-eight plays, thirty-eight languages. Nolan replied:

---

[30] Y. Nolan, personal interview, 15 December 2021. The full list is archived in Appendix 1 in Nolan's (2015) *Medicine Shows*. The chapter titled "Making Community" is Nolan's most recent first-hand written account of the process of making *Death of a Chief*.

[31] Richard Ouzounian. The reviewer for the *Globe and Mail*, J. Kelly Nestruck, has since retracted his review publicly.

> Our *Caesar* is mostly in Shakespeare's English, though there is a smattering of Ojibwe, a few words in Guna, Mohawk, and a whack of vocables. Native Earth is, of necessity, a pan-Indian theatre. Our constituency is primarily the urban Aboriginal population. Our artists come from all over ... What so many of us have in common is that we have not got our languages. (Nolan 2014, 227)

Bird passed. "We won't get away with doing a show that's mainly in English, just because it's not really fair on all the other companies who'd like to do that!" he wrote back. Setting aside for a moment the painful irony of a (white, male) representative of a major British theatre calling out an Algonquin woman for wanting to make a Shakespeare play in the language forced upon her community by the nation he represents – even as she reminds him that British cultural genocide means "*we have not got our languages*" – what has always stood out for me in this exchange is Bird's singular hang-up: words. He only hears the surface of language; he cannot hear Nolan's ontological claim, which precedes her linguistic one:

> Having said that, the piece is in our language in that it is crafted through a practice of Indigenous thought ... time is less linear, the ancestors are with us, the players grow right out of the land. Scenes happen simultaneously, layered. We – the company who crafted it – agreed to rituals and practices through a process of discussion and negotiation. But if you are looking for a Caesar in one Native language, we are not it. (Nolan 2014, 227)

Nolan tells Bird: our play does a thing – it makes a world, a world *we want*! – and we would like to share it with you. The hungry listener politely turns away. A more reciprocal listener, however, catches himself in his own bias. Reflecting on his experience of watching a workshop production before the NAC premiere and then revising his initial skepticism of using *Caesar* for decolonial purposes, Ric Knowles writes of Nolan's claim, on her own terms, to the power the other *Chief* reviewers seem so reluctant to relinquish:

> Yvette Nolan doesn't just claim that Shakespeare is universal, she lays claim, for herself and her community, to that universality: she claims the right of disenfranchised, colonized people to the authority and 'universality' that 'Shakespeare' represents in contemporary Western culture. (Knowles 2007, 63)

2.5 Community Telling

Reneltta Arluk's *Pawâkan* (2015–) inherits the power of Nolan's *Death of a Chief* to build a community from the bones of Shakespeare's stories, and then multiplies it. Like both *1939* and *Chief*, *Pawâkan* represents a specifically Indigenous version of PaR, a re-embodiment of colonial story via a community's shared cosmology, dramaturging survivance from the "scraps" of Shakespearean inheritance (Davies in press). *Pawâkan* has been in process since 2015, when it began as a two-week workshop with young people in the community of Frog Lake, Alberta; it now exists in two versions, both in constant conversation. One of these is a full-length play, adapted from *MacBeth* by Arluk and under contract with the Stratford Festival; the other is a community telling version, supported by the Canada Council for the Arts and the Banff Centre, and built by six actors with support from Arluk. In the latter form, *Pawâkan* has toured across Treaty 6 territory (which includes parts of the colonial province of Alberta), receiving a full production in Edmonton in early 2020. The story of *Pawâkan*'s doubled creation is the story of how Arluk strategically leveraged her various relationships with Stratford, the Canada Council, and the Banff Centre to use colonial Canadian arts money to transform *MacBeth* into a Plains Cree story, and then return it to Plains Cree communities as their own. *Pawâkan* is no less than an act of restitution: a return of colonial story, as contemporary resource, to Cree land.

Reneltta Arluk grew up in the Northwest Territories; she first encountered Shakespeare in junior high school. Like Nolan she was drawn to the playfulness of the language; an avid reader of all kinds of texts, she found "Shakespeare was saying words that were different than the words that I was reading in other places."[32] She later had the opportunity to attend the Centre for Indigenous Theatre in Toronto (as did Lauzon, years earlier when it was known as the Native Theatre School), where she developed a love for the sonnets, and for the rhythms of speaking the text aloud. She went on to become the first Indigenous woman to graduate from the University of Alberta's Bachelor of Fine Arts (BFA) acting programme, where she played the queen in *Two Noble Kinsmen*. After that, Arluk "never did Shakespeare [again]" because "I'm [from] the era where colorblind casting didn't exist."[33] Like so many equity-owed artists who find themselves frozen out of the Anglo-European classics, Arluk founded her own company, Akpik Theatre; it focuses on Northern Indigenous stories and was designed as an umbrella company to help funnel money and opportunities to other Indigenous artists (Ontario Performing Arts Presenting Network 2021). Working via Akpik to bring the arts home to underserved Northern communities, Arluk kept Shakespeare on hiatus – until Frog Lake.

Akpik's youth outreach programme was called *What's Your Story* in its early years; it brought

---

[32] R. Arluk, personal interview, 21 January 2022.
[33] R. Arluk, personal interview, 21 January 2022.

a singer, and a dancer or a spoken word artist, Indigenous male, IBPOC [Indigenous, Black, people of colour] female, and myself ... into different communities. And we would work with the youth centers, or schools, or friendship centres, whoever was the main youth gathering place. We would spend three to five days in the community and we would build stories from the youth involved themselves ... Then we would bring it together, like cabaret-style, and they would perform for their community. And it would be pay-what-you-can. (Ontario Performing Arts Presenting Network 2021)

Over time, however, Arluk realized that it was hard to work in depth with young people on such a tight time frame; she began to imagine what it would mean instead to go into a community for a couple of weeks, to do "deep relational work." Akpik was invited by Theatre Prospero to go to Frog Lake; the plan was initially for Arluk to work with students on *The Tempest*. Quickly, the students spoke back: they wanted to do *MacBeth*, and they wanted to include the Wihtiko (the Plains Cree version of Windigo, the hunger spirit) as central to their telling.

Frog Lake's school, like those in many Northern communities where governments have invested resources in Indigenous cultural spaces (if not in the basics, like paper towels in the bathrooms), had a cohort of students who knew their traditional stories, as well as a group of active, supportive Elders and community knowledge keepers. Arluk, along with Akpik associate director Barry Bilinsky (Métis, Cree, Ukranian), immediately gathered both students and Elders into a cross-generational collaboration. Wary about the huge energy (not unlike Shakespeare's!) that the Wihtiko carries, Arluk asked drama teacher Owen Morris to invite Elders to come to the workshop. Arluk imagined the Elders baulking at the students' request, cautioning them not to materialize such a dangerous figure as Wihtiko. But the Elders were eager to share their stories, and "the youth received them and then the youth shared with the Elders their own stories ... and then [they] talked about other creatures within the Treaty 6 area. . . . This is a really healthy community that knows its history and knows its cosmology, and that was really inspiring," Arluk remembers.[34]

The students' initial work received its first community telling in Frog Lake, with Elders like Gary Berland bringing ribbon shirts, sumptuous robes, and an intricate Wolverine headdress for the performers to wear. The production enacted a celebration of community stories and traditions hung on the scaffold of *MacBeth* – as Evelyne and her peers try to do with their community-visioning practice in *1939*. This was early 2015; that November, Arluk found herself seated next to Anthony Cimolino, artistic director at Stratford, during a playwright's retreat at the Festival (part of the Foerster Bernstein New Play Development Program). He asked her about her work in process and she told

---

[34] R. Arluk, personal interview, 21 January 2022.

him about *Pawâkan* – the Frog Lake artists had inspired her to take the play they built together to the next level. Cimolino was directing *MacBeth* in the upcoming Stratford season; they talked about the role of the witches, which Arluk was reimagining for *Pawâkan* as powerful Coyote-like figures who drive the action throughout the play. Called Wiyôyôwak, "literally the sound of howling in Cree," these figures are Arluk's own invention, representations of Cree spirituality and a reminder that good and bad co-exist in all cosmologies ("If we're going to keep our stories alive, we need to keep *all* of our stories alive," says Bilinsky [Moreno 2020, my emphasis]).

Arluk then began a process of mobilizing funding and support from a range of sources to enable further development of *Pawâkan*. Keira Loughran, then director of Stratford's Playwright's Lab and the most senior person of colour in the organization at the time, invited Arluk back to the Festival to work the script at the Lab. Roughly concurrently, Arluk applied to the Canada Council for the Arts' New Chapter program, "a special, one-time program created on the occasion of the 150th anniversary of Confederation" (Canada Council 2017) and designed to showcase contemporary Canadian diversity. She received the money. Also in 2017, Arluk was invited by Stratford to direct *The Breathing Hole*, a Festival commission by settler playwright Colleen Murphy (and starring, among others, Jani Lauzon). After *Breathing Hole* closed, Loughran organized a private reading of Arluk's script in process with both Indigenous and non-Indigenous members of the repertory company in residence. Not long after, Stratford formally commissioned Arluk to complete *Pawâkan* for a world premiere at the Festival.[35] *Pawâkan* was at the point of commission the largest investment the Playwright's Lab had ever made; the play in process also became, to some degree, Stratford's property (that is, under her contract's terms, Arluk was not permitted to stage it anywhere else before its Festival premiere). But she was also holding her New Chapter money; that money was earmarked for a community production and had terms and conditions of its own. She had to hack the funding system – and the "community telling" version was born. On Arluk's request, celebrated performing artist and York University professor Michael Greyeyes (Muskeg Lake Cree Nation) was named director for the Stratford full *Pawâkan*; meanwhile, Arluk hired half a dozen Indigenous actors from Western Canada and set to work with them tearing the play apart. Together they built a completely different version of Arluk's own story that could tour Treaty 6 territory, satisfy the Canada Council, not irk Stratford, and resonate fully in the communities Akpik Theatre serves.

---

[35] R. Arluk, personal interview, 21 January 2022.

The two versions of *Pawâkan* were always, of necessity, going to be different. The community telling version couldn't be two and a half hours long, and it certainly couldn't have an intermission. "We're going into communities that don't have much experience with theatre," Arluk notes; "at intermission, the community might just go home, lol. So what I did was I gave them the script," she says of her work with the actors she hired with her New Chapter funds.[36] She intended for them to story-tell her adaptation to build the community version, but she quickly came to realize that they didn't have traditional storytelling skills. (She chuckled, she says, at her own inherent bias: the actors relayed the action, but they didn't know yet how to put themselves into the story.) The team pivoted and their shared work on the community telling version became to learn the art of Indigenous storytelling together. Arluk ceded the play to the actors fully; they improvised from scene to scene and "[threw] my text away" with her blessing. Eventually, they had ninety minutes of shared story, built from the bones of Arluk's *Pawâkan*, itself built from the bones of Shakespeare's *MacBeth*. "I actually don't even really take credit for their community telling. It's told by the actors," Arluk says (see Figures 2 and 3).[37]

Figure 2 Allyson Pratt as Kâwanihot Iskwew and Aaron Wells as Macikosisân in *Pawâkan Macbeth (Community Telling Version)*. Photography by Donald Lee, The Banff Centre for Arts and Creativity.

---

[36] R. Arluk, personal interview, 21 January 2022.
[37] R. Arluk, personal interview, 21 January 2022.

Figure 3 Mitchell Saddleback as Otepwestamâkew in *Pawâkan Macbeth (Community Telling Version)*. Photography by Donald Lee, The Banff Centre for Arts and Creativity.

When Sheetala and I interviewed Arluk in late January 2022, she was at the Banff Centre, where she had recently taken up the role of director of Indigenous arts. It was there in January 2020 that she worked the community telling version with actors Sophie Merasty, Joel D. Montgrand, Allyson Pratt, Mitch Saddleback, Aaron Wells, and Kaitlyn Yott, going on to tour Treaty 6 territory just before the Covid-19 pandemic shut theatres.[38] At that same time, Greyeyes and his cast had been in residence at Banff too, working the full script. "So we took over Banff!" Arluk says delightedly; "we must have had 40 or 50 Indigenous artists at the Centre, all working on *Pawâkan*" – co-creating a new community story, a new *community*, with *MacBeth* as just another member of the team.

Making community from the bones of colonial text. Treating elite literary inheritance as shared sustenance. Arriving in the circle, together. These are some of the principles that the Indigenous women whose practices I've discussed here bring to their relationships with Shakespeare: their Shakespeare is a tool, a source of inspiration, a raw material for new making. A fellow researcher in a specifically Indigenous PaR exercise, his spirit is huge and it's dangerous, but held in community hands it can also be rich and revealing of this Turtle Island today. As we'll see next, these same principles – Shakespeare as

---

[38] See *Pawâkan* in a Covid-era Zoom telling, first broadcast on Facebook Live in 2021, at https://vimeo.com/513894867.

re/source in a democratized, playful creation room – apply for those dedicated to making Shakespeare intersectionally.

3 Intersectional Shakespeares

It's 10:45am on a bright, late fall morning in London. I have arrived at the NT Studio early; as an academic coming into artists' space, I want to make a good impression. It's the first day of what will be the final research and development (R&D) workshop for Emma Frankland's *Galatea* (Brighton Festival, 2023). I say "Frankland's *Galatea*," but Frankland would be quick to correct me. It's not her play, nor is it (sixteenth-century playwright) John Lyly's. This is *everyone's Galatea* – everyone in this room today; everyone who has participated in one of the previous R&D workshops or been involved in the project via fundraising, administration, or tech support; a whole community of makers from all backgrounds, disciplines, pronouns, colours, and histories.

I enter the Gov's room on the third floor and quickly realize that my being early is entirely unnecessary. In this space we come as we are able, and when we are able. At the first break, I sit to capture my initial impressions.

> I arrived early; Kemmy, Mydd and Nemo were already in the space. I introduced myself and we chatted easily; as others came in warmth built. Emma arrived shortly after 11am, full of hugs and smiles; around 11:15 or so we got started, low-key. Emma had us do five-minute meets with one person, then another; lots of talk about how we are, **where** we are as people right now. Then we went around and said names, pronouns, how we come to the project. People are open and warm and generous. The space feels very held.

If you've been in an inclusive rehearsal room before, some of the above might sound familiar. But this room is, literally, next level: it is a space where our collective differences *intentionally* form our foundation. We take nearly an hour to do welcomes; Andy Kesson, Frankland's long-time academic collaborator, calls this essential first act a process of levelling, making all in the space equally visible and valued.[39] Academics (like me and Kesson) and stage managers (like Nemo Martin) are considered as much a part of the creation process as actors or writers; in fact, our roles will become increasingly fluid as the week progresses.

Introductions over, Frankland offers us the room agreement.[40] It outlines our shared responsibilities, and it also talks about the ethos of our space. This is a space of process, one that is not geared toward making "a thing" but is about *doing things* in a way that challenges the hierarchizing, marginalizing backdrop

---

[39] A. Kesson, personal interview, 8 November 2021.
[40] This 2019 rehearsal room document is unpublished.

against which the theatre industry in the UK (and elsewhere) continues to operate. The vibe feels like a PaR experiment, a play space, and indeed the room agreement we're using this week has its origins in workshops Frankland hosted at the Stratford Festival in 2019, legacies of her landmark participation in the Stratford Lab's Engendering the Stage PaR workshop in 2018 (see Cockett and Gough in press). As she introduces the room agreement, Frankland credits two-spirit artists Cole Alvis [Michif] and Gein Wong [First Nations and Asian] for helping her to understand the harmful legacy of "Eurocentric ideals of excellence" in classical theatre production and reception.[41] According to those ideals, all labour in the creation room is supposed to be dedicated to making a "good" show. But: good according to whom? As Yvette Nolan reminds us (see Section 2), dominant culture gatekeepers (like reviewers, or artistic directors, or legacy funders) usually get to define what counts as "good," and thus they also get to shape public consensus about what kinds of bodies belong in what kinds of spaces – what or who "real" classical theatre, "real" Shakespeare, looks like. I look around me and realize that *this* room already looks incredibly different from our shared dominant culture norm: we are majority mixed race and of colour, and majority non-binary and trans.

In this section, I tell the stories of three creation processes across two different companies that work in a deliberately intersectional way: Emma Frankland and her expansive team of collaborators on *Galatea*, which received its premiere as a large-scale, community-oriented outdoor production in Shoreham-on-Sea in summer 2023; and Toronto-based Why Not Theatre, led by founding artistic director Ravi Jain and co-artistic director Miriam Fernandes. Why Not's *Prince Hamlet* (2017, 2019) and *R&J* (2021a) were co-created with the Deaf artist Dawn Jani Birley and the blind artist Alex Bulmer, respectively. Together, these companies offer a model for making work across racial, gendered, and ability intersections that begins with centring story on the embodied needs and living cultures of the most equity-owed artists in the room.

I begin by returning to some of the same ground we covered in Section 2; I end by thinking about the financial implications of making this kind of work and what those implications mean for the future of Shakespeare as an institution (to which we'll come in Section 4). After defining "intersectionality" and exploring its material contours, I look at how this section's creators build a room. How do they learn from their own errors and pivot to grow? What challenges arise as those with more privilege undertake to decentre themselves in the creation process? I then explore how these artists intentionally position early modern plays as collaborators rather than sources, tools to reach

---

[41] Galatea Research and Development Workshop #7 (20–24 November 2022).

community goals – and fiscal ones. Lyly's *Galatea* is present here alongside Shakespeare's superstars because, as Kesson notes, Shakespeare borrowed much from Lyly but straightened many of his queer edges. Those straightened edges now mean that we perceive the culture(s) for which Shakespeare stands to be more straight than queer, too, which encourages the Shakespeare industry to remain broadly conservative in the kinds of ideas and bodies it platforms.[42] To turn back to Lyly is to imagine a queerer, more gender-fluid early modern future for artists of all kinds; similarly, to keep the currency of *Hamlet* and *Romeo and Juliet* in the mix is to bank some of Shakespeare's capital explicitly to fund the kinds of artists who will make that future a reality.

3.1 Intersectionality: Mobilizing the Metaphor

Dawn Jani Birley first met Ravi Jain on a video call. She asked if he wanted a sign language interpreter; he said no: they could figure out how to speak together. This made a deep impression on Birley; it marked Jain as a hearing person "that you can work with."[43] Birley asked Jain which lens he intended to bring to *Prince Hamlet*, in which Birley appears as both translator/adapter of the text and a culturally Deaf Horatio. Was he aiming for an inclusive lens or an intersectional one? He didn't know. She explained:

> when we look at things from an inclusive lens, or inclusion, that's when the majority does something for the other. The majority sees *me* as the problem. . . . And so they approach [the work] by helping me to overcome that problem. Intersectionality is very different: we as a group, as a collective, work together to solve the issue that is *external* from the person.[44]

Birley's intersectionality mobilizes the term to describe a process for mutual theatrical creation that can bring Deaf and hearing artists together to challenge what dominant theatre culture perceives as an intractable Deaf–hearing divide. Developed over the course of her master's degree in the UK, Birley's intersectionality builds on the work of Kimberlé Williams Crenshaw, the legal scholar who brought the term to critical prominence in two landmark papers. Crenshaw's intersectionality derives from the historical legacy of Black feminist thought (Carastathis 2016, 124) and is grounded in the experiences of Black women enmeshed in the US legal system. In her 1989 paper, Crenshaw uses two metaphors – a traffic intersection and a basement – to demonstrate how these women's experiences are doubly discounted because "both are predicated on a discrete set of experiences [being a woman *or* being Black] that often does not

---

[42] A. Kesson, personal interview, 8 November 2021.
[43] D. Jani Birley and C. Horne, personal interview, 7 March 2022.
[44] D. Jani Birley and C. Horne, personal interview, 7 March 2022.

accurately reflect the interaction of race and gender" in shaping their lives and their experiences of harm (Crenshaw 1989, 140).

Think of an intersection, Crenshaw suggests in that paper: traffic comes from all angles, and if a car in the middle of the intersection is hit, it may be hit from any angle – or from multiple angles, compounding the injuries sustained (Crenshaw 1989, 149). This is the metaphor of intersectionality that has endured in simplified form, leading to our popular understanding of the word as meaning multiple identities = multiple forms of oppression. However, in the same paper, Crenshaw offers a second metaphor. Imagine a basement: folks experiencing discrimination are stacked shoulder upon shoulder, with those who experience multiple, compounding forms of discrimination on the bottom, and those disadvantaged by only one form (say, Black, cis- men, or white, straight women) hitting the ceiling. Let's say a hatch in the ceiling opens and that first layer squeezes up; the structure can then celebrate its capacity for inclusivity. Those from below with the most relative privilege can join those above who have always benefited from proximity to existing power structures; thereby, those structures endure. Meanwhile, the folks on whom the entire structure literally rests are left in the dark below.

In her 2016 reassessment of Crenshaw's work, Anna Carastathis recovers two important valences of the original "intersectionality." First, intersectionality is designed to be "a provisional concept, meant to get us to think about *how* we think" (Carastathis 2016, 4). Second, in its provisional status, intersectionality requires a politics of coalition (Carastathis 2016, 5), an active *rethinking together* of how we have systemically been taught to imagine the world. Understanding intersectionality as ongoing, provisional, coalitional labour designed to move us toward the collective dismantling of harmful social structures also means, for Carastathis, that we must be prepared to become "disoriented" as we unlearn our own biases and expectations: "in order to transform our thinking, let alone institutionalized practices, our current axiomatic assumptions, cognitive habits, and unreflective premises have to be at once engaged and disrupted" (Carastathis 2016, 108–9).

Carastathis's rereading of Crenshaw through intersectionality's provisional and coalitional dimensions rematerializes Crenshaw's original metaphors. It reclaims their radical potential as *a doing*: as the work of *intersecting with* others and adjusting as needed, not the satisfaction of being willing to "include" others without adjusting at all. This is also Birley's intersectionality. It heeds Crenshaw's (1989) call to "place those who currently are marginalized in the centre" in order best "to resist efforts to compartmentalize experiences and undermine potential collective action" (Carastathis 2016, 167). After all, centring those normally marginalized works safely at an intersection only when we fundamentally rethink what an intersection should look like, who it should be for: think a pedestrian scramble crossing, not a highway interchange. Only when we make the metaphor literal, a matter of real bodies sharing space together, can properly equitable alternatives appear.

3.2 Building the Room

Many participants in Emma Frankland's creation rooms have described the very same feelings I share above: a sense of being encouraged to bring as much or as little of themselves into the room as they feel able to do; of feeling included in a level playing space rather than ranked according to the privilege traditionally attached to theatre vocations (director, then actors, then designers . . . tech support and academics quietly at the back); of feeling that the differences we bring (racial, ability, or gendered, social or in terms of work or life experience) are assets, not detriments. So, when I sat down with Frankland to speak to her about her work on *Galatea*, I asked her about how she builds and holds this space.

She talked first about deep listening: about what it has meant for her, over the multi-year *Galatea* creation process, to discover from others what they need in a secure, functional room, and then to treat the room-building process as one of unlearning her own assumptions. Frankland grew up in an artistic family with lots of Shakespeare around, but she first met John Lyly and *Galatea* (c. 1584–8) at Shakespeare's Globe during the *Read Not Dead* project that ran in the mid-2010s. Having recently studied acting at master's level at the Royal Central School of Speech and Drama, and having also recently begun transitioning, Frankland's perspective toward Lyly was tentative. She was trained to engage with *Galatea*, a Shakespeare-adjacent early modern text, "very much through a cis white patriarchal lens," and yet she was also beginning to feel "the slow decline in my involvement with organizations such as the Globe and with the classical performance world in general" that occurred alongside her coming out as trans.[45] In the play, aspects of which Shakespeare borrowed for later plays including *As You Like It* and *The Tempest*, two virgins are disguised as boys and sent to the forest to avoid being sacrificed to the god Neptune's monster Agar; in the forest they fall in love, and at the play's end, thanks to the goddess Venus, they are invited to live happily ever after. As Frankland began to build "her own relationship" to the early moderns via *Galatea*, she explored the play's latent queerness; she found in Lyly a trans ally and trans stories in his characters (Frankland and Kesson 2019). The play became a bridge between the box-office classical theatre world that had decided it was not "for" Frankland anymore and

---

[45] E. Frankland, personal interview, 2 November 2021.

the world of contemporary experimental performance in which her art practice since transitioning has largely lived (see Frankland 2019a).

The first *Galatea* R&D workshop, in 2016, was supported by the Jerwood Foundation. Frankland decided that the room should include artists she would normally collaborate with as part of her contemporary practice, rather than trained actors familiar with classical spaces:

> I always like to have the potential for people to bring their lived identities into projects. Not as a requirement of bringing your most traumatic element to the stage, but as an offer. So the room was consciously built of artists who had their own practice. And also generally speaking, their practice spoke about some element of our identity that was marginalized. So, we ended up with a very intersectional room with many people who'd never encountered early modern text before. It was very joyful.[46]

That first room allowed for a series of crucial discoveries that have shaped both *Galatea*'s development and Frankland's spacing process ever since. Because of the range of lived differences in the room, and because all of the participants in the room had received the explicit offer to bring both their artistic expertise *and* their whole selves into the room, the team were able to have frank conversations about the play's queer and trans dimensions, its imbrications with race and racism, and the ways in which it codes for Deaf as well as hearing experience.

All subsequent R&D periods shifted or added new artists and collaborators according to the dimensions of difference that had been explored in earlier workshops. Frankland treated these periods as opportunities for her to learn more deeply about her white and ableist privilege, as well as about trans experience across intersections beyond her own. Thanks to discussions with collaborators of colour, the team has reckoned with the language of "fairness" (i.e., whiteness) in the play and rewritten passages or eliminated phrases that do not serve Black and people of colour (POC) actors. Thanks to ongoing collaboration with a group of Deaf actors including Nadia Nadarajah, the team has also moved away from the notion of "integrating" British Sign Language (BSL)-speaking actors into the project and toward "making an equitable production that works for the Deaf actors and hearing actors equally" (akin to Birley's practice). The process, as Frankland describes it, "hasn't been straightforward," but it has been marked by her "taking ownership over" both successes and mistakes, as well as over the work required to produce genuine equity in the room.[47]

Built from her willingness to become disoriented, and her commitment to listen and learn from her own mistakes, Frankland's room encourages the very

---

[46] E. Frankland, personal interview, 2 November 2021.
[47] E. Frankland, personal interview, 2 November 2021.

same from its members, so that we all may be moved to think carefully: is this world we are building together a place we really want to be? The room agreement we used at the NT Studio in November 2022 reads as follows:

To recognise our intersections/differences while maintaining community we will:

- ○ *Give permission to disagree*
- ○ *Where relevant, socially position ourselves*
- ○ *Hold affinity spaces if desired [spaces in which members of a specific group, for example Deaf or trans participants, can go to be with each other, recalibrate, reaffirm security and safety]*

- − *We give permission to leave*
- − *We will take care of the group and ourselves*
- − *We will not use language that is problematic or appropriative*
- − *There will be confidentiality (stories can be shared, identities will be protected)*
- − *We can use the 'oops/ouch' tool*
- − *It's our responsibility to articulate our needs where possible*
- − *We are moving towards decolonising space/language (making space for all ways of identifying)*
- − *Moving through discomfort but adjusting before harm.*

Both specific and highly flexible, the agreement holds in tension two promises: that we will take care of one another, which includes actively taking care of ourselves; and that we will create the conditions possible for us to become uncomfortable with each other while avoiding harm. The "oops/ouch" tool offers an ideal example of this tension in practice. If someone causes accidental harm – for example, a misgendering – and then realizes the mistake, they can say "oops" to signal responsibility-taking. They to whom harm is caused may then say "ouch," which acts as acknowledgement and as permission to take the lead on next steps. Both parties can speak more, if they feel this is needed or wanted, but it is not required. The tool allows that small harms may happen without intention but reparations can still be made *with* intention; the community can move on, simultaneously taking responsibility and offering care.

Long-time academic collaborator Andy Kesson describes Frankland's room as "somewhat counterintuitive": Frankland's ethos encompasses both a drive toward community and its simultaneous disruption, a deep safety coupled with genuine discomfort.[48] It is typical, he notes, for Frankland to spend time building trust and security in the room, and then to send a small group of participants away

---

Figure 4 Emma Frankland and Kemi Coker mess around during group warm-up activities. *Galatea* Research and Development Workshop #7, NT Studio, 20–24 November 2022. Photo by Joe Twigg.

"with an entirely contradictory task" to work on. Later, she will invite the rogue group back, specifically "to disturb the world" the main room has been building by introducing unexpected conflict. The goal is to produce "a community building itself up and having an understanding of who they are, and then being forced to redefine itself."[49] The healthy navigation of difference and the development of skills that make a community more porous, more flexible, more resilient, and ultimately more open: this is the work of Frankland's creation room (see Figure 4).

3.3 The Art of Starting Over

Hamlet was not just putting on a play. It's deeper than that.
It's a political statement.

Ravi Jain[50]

Pauline Oliveros defines "deep listening" as taking in, and then acting upon, what those around you tell you they need. Kathleen Fitzpatrick, in resonance

---

[49] A. Kesson, personal interview, 8 November 2021.
[50] M. Fernandes and R. Jain, personal interview, 7 December 2021.

with Robinson's work on Indigenous sound practice, describes hearing as "something that happens to the ear," but listening as "a cognitive act in which one must participate" (Fitzpatrick 2021, 74). Taken seriously, listening hails us, demands that we *do something*. Fitzpatrick quotes Krista Tippett: "Generous listening . . . involves a kind of vulnerability – a willingness to be surprised, to let go" (Fitzpatrick 2021, 76).

With Miriam Fernandes, Ravi Jain is co-artistic director of Why Not Theatre in Toronto, and he is an important ally in this section's story. His creation room, like Frankland's, is a product of deep listening: he centres those who are typically not given the opportunity to create on their own terms in dominant culture spaces because of systemic oppressions and the barriers erected by elite tradition. Jain founded Why Not in 2007, after returning to Canada from years abroad training and working. Even with credentials from the London Academy of Music and Dramatic Art (LAMDA), New York University, and the Lecoq school, Jain found himself "hitting hard systemic racism in a massive way" as he sought work in the industry.[51] He built Why Not on the principle of access: creating the kind of work he found exciting by giving artists like himself opportunities to exercise their creativity freely. He maintains Why Not's profile and industry currency, as well as its war chest for artist uplift, in part by turning to audience-friendly fare (*A Brimful of Asha*), mythical classics (*Mahabharata*), and blockbuster Shakespeare. Jain, a Canadian-born South Asian and a drama kid from the start, regards Shakespeare as "Kleenex": a bankable resource that enables his company to support other creators, as well as a place to learn, play, and reinvent as an artist. Regardless of project, profile, or producing partners, however, all of Jain's projects begin with Why Not's guiding question: *who gets to tell the story?*

Hamlet was Why Not's first show, cut and directed by Jain, in 2007; "ten years later" he was interested in discovering what the company had learned, not by remounting it but by making it "again, but better."

> [I asked], who are people that would never be cast in this show? Christine [Horne] as Hamlet. No brainer. No professional production . . . has had a female *Hamlet* [in Canada circa 2017]. And then, you know, it started ticking . . . Karen Robinson [Black] understudied Gertrude at Stratford but didn't play Gertrude. So, like, just ticking off these people who I would never see in these roles.[52]

Working across the ability spectrum hadn't been on Jain's radar until he found himself at a US conference focused on equity, diversity, and inclusion.

---

[51] M. Fernandes and R. Jain, personal interview, 7 December 2021.

[52] M. Fernandes and R. Jain, personal interview, 7 December 2021.

Via Black creator Lisa Karen Cox, Jain got in touch with Birley, and the meeting I described earlier in this section took place. The wheels were in motion; importantly, though, the vision wasn't fixed. "I didn't have a clue what we were gonna make!" Jain exclaims. For *R&J*, Jain worked the script with frequent Why Not collaborator Christine Horne; he was interested in exploring "the tension between young and old [in the play] ... what is this future that we're fighting for?" But *R&J* only began in earnest with the casting of fourteen-year-old Eponine Lee as Juliet and blind artist Alex Bulmer as the Friar. "The people will help determine what the project ends up being," Jain notes.[53]

Why Not's four-year span of work on *Prince Hamlet* (2017–19) and then *R&J* (2021) makes a superb case study in what Frankland describes as the "not straightforward-ness" – the well-intentioned but inevitably error-strewn challenge – of working in a genuinely intersectional way. *Prince Hamlet* was created twice: in 2017, which Christine Horne describes as "getting the idea of the show," and again in 2019, which she calls "THE show" (Birley describes the span between these productions as "a world of difference").[54]

At the start of the 2017 process, the room worked in separate spheres, only one of which included Birley; Jain anticipated being able to integrate the two later in the process. Birley pressed Jain on this separation because, from her culturally Deaf perspective, none was plausible within the world of the play: "as I began to analyze the story, I thought, if Horatio and Hamlet are best friends, then what does that mean? If Hamlet and I, Deaf and hearing, had grown up together and continue to be best friends then we must be signing to each other to communicate."[55]

Further, Birley reasoned, if Horatio has long been part of Hamlet's life, then the King and the Queen, too, must have some knowledge of sign language; so may Ophelia and Laertes, and even members of the guard. Birley recalls bringing this up often in the first few weeks of rehearsal only to be "put on hold" while work continued on lines and devising in the other spaces in the room. Jain asked her to comment on the emerging first half around week three. "I looked at it and said, 'I don't know what they're saying," Birley recalls; Jain had scored the scenes physically and visually according to his hearing perspective, aiming for universal readability. Birley's response was: "maybe, right, if

[53] M. Fernandes and R. Jain, personal interview, 7 December 2021.

[54] D. Jani Birley and C. Horne, personal interview, 7 March 2022. Birley was introduced to Shakespeare in high school; she attended a public school (not a school for Deaf children) thanks to her parents' stringent activism, and she credits teacher and mentor Colette Hugs for encouraging her work on the plays.

[55] D. Jani Birley and C. Horne, personal interview, 7 March 2022.

you can *hear [what they are saying] too*, but to me I don't see what you're trying to tell me!"[56]

The above paints a familiar picture of what happens when you centre difference in a way that is more tokenistic than holistic, regardless of good intentions. But it's also a familiar picture because, for those of us approaching intersectional work from learned dominant culture perspectives, mistakes are inevitable – they are, as Alex Bulmer notes, both expected and necessary in the process of learning to work well across vectors of difference.[57] Jain's response to Birley was telling: "Okay! We go back to the drawing board!" Birley notes how, again and again, Jain was willing to recognize his mistakes, own them, and then *just start over*. She describes the above moment in the *Prince Hamlet* process as pivotal: "I had to ask, Who do you think this audience is? Is [the show] for both Deaf and hearing audience members? If so, you have to think of how both [groups of] patrons are going to experience it."[58] She explained that, in its current iteration, their work in progress pointed to her, a Deaf spectator, as a problem to solve in the dramaturgy of the text. What they needed for an intersectional production was a solution to the real problem: how both hearing and Deaf audience members could encounter the story on equal, shared terms.

This realization spurred the team to change course completely. In the resulting final production (Why Not Theatre 2017), sometimes Deaf audiences were privileged to understand what was going on in a way that hearing audiences could not, and vice versa. However, to ensure that this experience of knowing or not knowing was shared equitably across a bilingual platform – and to do so with less than two weeks until opening – Birley's labour had to push into overdrive. Horne recalls: "Dawn would have to teach us everything! Not only ... being like sort of the Deaf cultural consultant for the production and doing all the translation, but ... anything any of us had to sign, Dawn had to take time to teach us. ... that was a ton of work."[59]

All of those I interviewed about *Prince Hamlet* acknowledged how excessive Birley's labour was in 2017, but that acknowledgement also fed a deep sense of respect and a spur to learning. Ahead of the 2019 rebuild, several members of the cast took the time to learn some ASL, and Why Not funded a full three weeks of rehearsal (versus the one-week norm for a remount) so that Birley might revisit her original ASL translation to deepen the story for Deaf spectators. Horne learned significant ASL, enabling Horatio and Hamlet to really begin to play with the language and each other; Horne's initiative came directly

---

[56] D. Jani Birley and C. Horne, personal interview, 7 March 2022.

[57] A. Bulmer, personal interview, 26 January 2022.

[58] D. Jani Birley and C. Horne, personal interview, 7 March 2022.

[59] D. Jani Birley and C. Horne, personal interview, 7 March 2022.

Figure 5 Dawn Jani Birley (left), Rick Roberts (centre), and Christine Horne in Why Not Theatre's *Prince Hamlet*. Photography by Bronwen Sharp.

from her respect for Birley's initial investment of time and labour. She recalls: "it felt like I have to do what I can to, to meet Dawn, to bring what I can … there's only so much I'm going to be able to learn but I have to do my best to be able to come back and balance those skills" (see Figure 5).[60]

Ravi Jain likes to ask his collaborators, "I need you to be your fullest creative self. What do I need to do [to enable that]?"[61] From *Prince Hamlet*, Why Not "learned a lot" about working intersectionally across ability, and Jain and Horne put their learning into practice curating the room for *R&J* (Why Not Theatre 2021a).[62] I'll speak in more detail about *R&J* in Section 3.4, but for now it's worth highlighting changes that the company made to their creation process so that Alex Bulmer (blind) and Eponine Lee (a minor) could both show up *and just make theatre*. Why Not produced *R&J* with the Stratford Festival, and Jain used his power and privilege as a sought-after theatre maker to ensure that conversations between Why Not and Stratford took place well ahead of rehearsals to guarantee safety provisions for Bulmer and Lee both onstage and off. Horne worked with Lee on the text ahead of time to help her feel prepared coming into rehearsal with a group of adult actors. Blind consultants and youth consultants were hired to anticipate Lee's and Bulmer's needs ahead of time. Jain and Horne cut *Romeo and Juliet* for the rehearsal process, but provided several versions of

---

[60] D. Jani Birley and C. Horne, personal interview, 7 March 2022.

[61] M. Fernandes and R. Jain, personal interview, 7 December 2021.

[62] C. Horne, D. Jemmott, and E. Lee, personal interview, 24 January 2022.

the possible script as offerings, granting the cast strong creative agency in developing the final cut. The room contained a "question box" that invited artists to share thoughts privately with Jain and Horne as needed. The result? The team felt "entirely safe,"[63] empowered (Dante Jemmott), never judged (Lee).[64] Tom Rooney, the only Stratford veteran in the cast, described to me the way the centring of Bulmer's and Lee's respective needs disrupted expectations about who gets to take up space in rehearsal, who gets to contribute to storytelling in a place like Stratford: "Voice people and movement people often come into rehearsal and feel like they need to be a little bit invisible," he told me, "whereas in this situation, they had to come in and say, 'I, Tom, am in the room' [so Alex would know]. There was something very wonderful and very democratic about that."[65]

3.4 "I Am Not a Metaphor": The Text as Collaborator

Like Birley, Alex Bulmer also tells a great story about the conversation she had with Ravi Jain when he phoned to ask her if she'd like to play the Friar in *R&J*. Jain asked Bulmer about the famous lines with which Mercutio and Benvolio tease Romeo in Act 2, scene 1. Did she think "love is blind" was an ableist metaphor?[66] "And I said, well if you think of blindness as like an absence or unawareness, which is how most people use the metaphor, then yes of course it's ableist. But if you mean blindness as infinite possibility, then I wouldn't call it ableist."[67]

The Mercutio–Benvolio exchange codes for both readings: Benvolio references darkness as the safest place for love to find some freedom in a combative society organized around surveillance, while Mercutio claims that blind love "cannot hit the mark," presumably because, without its eyes, it is disoriented. Bulmer's "infinite possibility," like Benvolio's take, does not begin from the assumption that darkness is a problem, so she countered Jain's question with an analogy of her own. Imagine you throw a rock into a pond. If you are sighted, your journey starts when you pick up the rock; it ends when the rock hits the water. If you are blind, "it starts when you hear PLOP into the water, and then you imagine ripples ... and then all of a sudden your imagination fills with a whole story."[68] (See also Why Not Theatre 2021b.)

---

[63] A. Bulmer, personal interview, 26 January 2022.

[64] C. Horne, D. Jemmott, and E. Lee, personal interview, 24 January 2022.

[65] T. Rooney, personal interview, 30 January 2022.

[66] "Benvolio: Come, he hath hid himself among these trees, / To be consorted with the humorous night. / Blind is his love, and best befits the dark. Mercutio: "If love be blind, love cannot hit the mark" (ll. 33–6).

[67] A. Bulmer, personal interview, 26 January 2022.

[68] A. Bulmer, personal interview, 26 January 2022.

Alex Bulmer first met Shakespeare as a small child, attending Shakespeare Club with her beloved grandmother; it was while she was in rehearsals for *A Midsummer Night's Dream* at Bishop's University in 1987 that she flew home for the eye appointment at which she was diagnosed with retinitis pigmentosa, a degenerative condition. When she returned to school, her director Greg Tuck rolled with the challenge, fitting her with a headlamp and transforming her into a firefly; it's this "way of thinking" – seeing "creative possibilities in disability" – that has shaped Bulmer's interactions with Shakespeare ever since.[69] When Bulmer arrived at the first *R&J* work-shop in March 2021, she discovered what a huge impact her "love is blind" thoughts had had on Jain. He'd developed a provisional concept for the show in which Bulmer as the Friar would tell the story from her perspective, performing on an empty stage with only a chair. The first time they tried this out, Jain asked Bulmer if she had "an impulse" to move around. I do, she said, "but I don't know where I am!" Jain immediately realized that the concept as he had imagined it – helping a sighted audience to "experience" love's blindness through the Friar's blindness – could never work for her, the living blind performer, "because my whole world is about making contact with things."[70] She went on to explain that "love is blind" may be a familiar metaphor and one worth unpacking, but "I am not a metaphor" (Why Not Theatre 2021b).

A metaphor is "a figure of speech in which a name or descriptive word or phrase is transferred to an object or action different from, but analogous to, [it]" (OED n.d.). We associate metaphor with great poetry, but what that association often forgets is that metaphors are based on simultaneous ostension and elision. They lift one thing to our view in a new way, while diminishing or even erasing the materiality of the comparator thing: "love is blind" takes the meaning of blindness for granted. Metaphor thus emerges from linguistic privilege: to "get it," you need to be fluent in the metaphor's language – you need to know what "blind" means, and the meaning that most regularly comes to mind belongs to the dominant culture. Alex Bulmer's body in the space of *R&J* physically changed the meaning of the story's central metaphor and thus the orientation from which the story itself could be told. Jain and Horne, true to form and expectation, immediately started all over again. "The version of *R&J*" that they had to build, Horne recalls, needed to be the one that "facilitates [Alex] playing this part": that meant (1) The Friar is always in a place very familiar to him and (2) the Friar never leaves the stage (to accommodate Covid-19 safety rules in place at the time).[71] The team settled on the

---

[69] A. Bulmer, personal interview, 26 January 2022.
[70] A. Bulmer, personal interview, 26 January 2022.
[71] C. Horne, D. Jemmott, and E. Lee, personal interview, 24 January 2022.

Figure 6 Dante Jemmott (left) as Romeo and Alex Bulmer as the Friar in *R+J* (Stratford Festival, Why Not Theatre 2021a). Photograph by David Hou.

Friar's lodging as the set; designer Julie Fox collaborated with Bulmer in order to build a rich physical world that mirrored Bulmer's use of her own private space.[72] The rest of the process resembled devising more than rehearsal. Each day brought new discoveries, followed by a new script from Jain and Horne the next morning; on many occasions, recalls Dante Jemmott, there was no acting, just a lot of discussion about what story of any given scene the group wanted to tell. The Friar's relationship with Romeo and Juliet became central to the team's concept for the play, which focused on intergenerational learning and the development of an ethically sustainable world; much of that story was inspired by improvising with one another, and much of it developed gesturally rather than through language (see Figure 6). Jemmott recalls rehearsing the moment when the Friar explains to Romeo that he is banished:

> . . . no words were exchanged. I was on the floor and Alex was on the floor. And she was just reaching out to me. And then we broke some COVID rules, and she touched me. And that's all that happened [in the rehearsal]. There was this intimacy about that scene that was . . . just there for me for the entire rehearsal process and the entire run of the show. Because of that rehearsal.[73]

---

[72] A. Bulmer, personal interview, 26 January 2022.
[73] C. Horne, D. Jemmott, and E. Lee, personal interview, 24 January 2022.

The creation of *R&J*, like the creation of *Prince Hamlet*, exemplifies what can emerge when, as Fernandes puts it, you "centre another culture" and that culture's uniquely embodied experience of language, poetry, and metaphor in the making of Shakespeare instead of centering "the text" (much as *1939* did as it indigenized Helena's story and translated its poetry into Mohawk; see Section 2). For both *Prince Hamlet* and *R&J*, Fernandes explains, "the portal in wasn't language first ... [and] that allowed us to meet the language [of the play] in a different way."[74] The physical requirements of the encultured bodies on stage became each production's defining parameters, which in turn determined which elements of "the text" were of value and which should be disregarded. Birley and Jain chose to translate or discard metaphors from *Hamlet* depending on how they best saw fit to convey a metaphor's intentions; often, words were simply not needed to say what the story wanted to communicate. Birley developed an entirely visual representation of Gertrude's speech after Ophelia's drowning, one that disregarded *both* English *and* ASL and chose instead to act out Gertrude's emotions in a physical register unique to the production. The resulting scene "has most thoroughly stuck in people's minds," as Birley notes; it is appreciated equally by ASL speakers and by those who prize the original poetry. In 2019, with much more ASL in the room, the team cut more and more of the Shakespeare, working the story through hands, gestures, and facial expressions; ASL allowed the team to "liberate" Horatio's story from the overdetermined text of *Hamlet*. Birley explains:

> Sign Language provides some liberation, some freedom, to express ... spoken language is more constraining in some ways. As Deaf people who are signers, we have the capacity to reveal our emotions through our hands and our faces. If you can show the emotion then you have conveyed it, and I think that in Shakespeare those stories offer us that opportunity to connect through the emotion.[75]

3.5 Remapping the Past, Funding the Future

After the first break on our first day at the NT Studio, Frankland introduces the room to the story of *Galatea*. She tells us, "This is a play about a town that has forgotten how to love, and a monster is coming." Ferocious Agar comes every five years to take the town's "fairest" virgin; Galatea and Phyllida are young people the community reads as female, and this year they are monster fodder. Their dads both decide, independently, to dress them as boys and send them into the woods to hide. There, Galatea and Phyllida discover that they love one another; they

[74] M. Fernandes and R. Jain, personal interview, 7 December 2021.
[75] D. Jani Birley and C. Horne, personal interview, 7 March 2022.

also discover the goddess Diana, who presides over a community of equals where love, not "fairness," is the currency. At the play's end, Galatea and Phyllida are still in love, even though unmasked to the town as ladies. Venus saves the day; she declares "I like well and allow it," and states that she will "turn one" of the pair into a man. But we never learn who is changed – or if anyone is (Frankland and Joy 2023, 76–7).

This is the story behind the text, and we dwell with it before Frankland hands out any paper. She talks about how, over various R&D periods focused on clues about Blackness in the play, the trans potential of the lovers, the town's structure as a community, and the role of Deaf experience in the play, the creation team has come to understand that *Galatea* isn't a Deaf or trans or Black story – all of these stories exist *within* its world, but above all it is a play about a community filled with people terrified of difference. When we finally get our scenes for the week, Frankland is clear: the fact that "the text" is now here does not mean that it is suddenly the boss (I think of Lauzon: a text surrounded by present, human stories). Frankland then explains that the text is meant as a point of reference only; she says that it will be the job of the play and the characters to bend and flex around us, not the other way (see Figure 7).

Figure 7 Emma Frankland (foreground) and Subira Joy explore "the text" during the *Galatea* Research and Development Workshop #7, NT Studio, 20–24 November 2022. Photo by Joe Twigg.

How much do we know of the *context* that we revere, when we revere the texts of Shakespeare and company? Andy Kesson tells me that our assumptions about the look and feel of the early modern period, based in colonial Bardolatry, are tenacious but generally wrong: "we [think we] know what historical theatre looks like, and what contemporary classical theatre looks like, and [they both] look like Shakespeare."[76] Recent research (including practice-based research) by Kesson and Frankland, Sawyer Kemp, Lucy Munro, Natasha Corda, Clare McManus, Callan Davies, Peter Cockett, Melinda Gough, and many others reveals a very different, much queerer early modern theatre ecology, one that rested to a significant extent on the power and influence of women, non-binary, and transgender folks (Davies 2018; Frankland 2019b; Cockett and Gough in press). Lyly wrote for a company owned by a woman and often named his plays after women – and those plays don't end with marriages. "Shakespeare has fixed us with a world in which most plays are named after male characters, and in the case of comedies are moving towards heterosexual marriage," Kesson notes, but "it's possible to entirely remap our sense of diversity in the period" by looking away from Shakespeare and toward a much broader and more socially and sexually diverse web of early modern writing than we've previously admitted into theatrical consciousness.[77] At the end of *Sapho and Phao*, Lyly's prequel to *Galatea*, Sapho takes Cupid hostage and declares love "a toy for ladies only," a "radical agenda" that sets the stage for *Galatea* to celebrate the social and political viability of two women-presenting humans' love for one another.[78] So, when Frankland asserts in the studio the importance of our contemporary agency as *Galatea* co-creators, she is not only positioning Lyly as a queer, Deaf, and trans "ally" and his text as our collaborator; she and Kesson are practicing a performative remapping that reveals a fresh theatre history, one that doesn't look like Shakespearean heteropatriarchy at all.

Frankland and Kesson's selection of *Galatea* is a clear, deliberate political choice; so too are Why Not's choices of *Hamlet* and *Romeo and Juliet*. *Galatea* invites us to reflect on why Shakespeare should be our early modern default when so many other, more gender-(and race- and ability-)inclusive options exist in the canon; meanwhile, *Prince Hamlet* and *R&J* invite us to see and hear our "default" Shakespeares through new languages, perspectives, and embodied practices. Why Not's choice of the heavy hitters is political for another reason, too: because they sell. Jain is not shy about articulating Why Not's economic

---

[76] A. Kesson, personal interview, 8 November 2021.
[77] A. Kesson, personal interview, 8 November 2021. See also https://beforeshakespeare.com/, curated by Kesson, and *Gender on the Transnational Early Modern Stage, Then and Now: A Performance as Research Approach*, edited by Cockett and Gough (in press).
[78] A. Kesson, personal interview, 8 November 2021.

calculus because when the company's *Hamlet* goes on tour, and when *R&J* is co-produced by a well-resourced institution like the Stratford Festival, it means more resources for the company to funnel into accessibility and support. It also means money to direct at its community programs like RISER,[79] designed to give independent, equity-owed artists the space, time, and professional administrative assistance to make whatever they want on their own terms.[80] Why Not's policy of "share everything" directly addresses the fact that the labour of making genuinely equitable theatre (and *especially* genuinely equitable classical theatre, with its large casts and multiple settings) requires extensive material support to ensure that artists are fairly compensated for all of their work, including unexpected "diversity work"; to ensure that accessibility mechanisms are in place for all members of the company who need them; and to ensure that creation and rehearsal timelines can compensate for the need to throw out ideas that cannot work for all company members, and start again.

Galatea was ambitious in scale, and Kesson and Frankland were deeply committed to ensuring equity and accessibility for all: their resource requirements were extensive indeed. In final production, *Galatea* included over 100 crew members at an outdoor site that featured multiple stage areas, food trucks, and a festival-like pre-show; with numerous trans, non-binary, Black, Indigenous, people of colour (BIPOC), Deaf, and disabled team members participating, the creative leadership had to support different groups of participants with often very different access needs, some of which were emergent as the rehearsal period continued and circumstances (including the weather) intervened. For independent artists and smaller companies (both of which are more likely to be, or to include, equity-owed folks), the financial support for such resource requirements can't just come from the "top" down; it needs to be negotiated across partner companies in advance and supplemented with grants from government and/or academic organizations, making the accessibility supply chain extremely contingent. From the beginning, Frankland and Kesson were adamant that *Galatea* could be professionally staged only if that production were fully accessible and safe for all makers, and they spent significant chunks of time over the production's seven-plus-year incubation period applying for grant and residency support to get the next few steps down the road. *Galatea* could finally be imagined as a full-scale production when Frankland and Kesson won major funding from both Arts Council England (ACE) and the Arts and Humanities Research Council (AHRC) in 2022, accompanied by

---

[79] Find more information on RISER at https://whynot.theatre/work/riser/.

[80] Since their collaboration on *Prince Hamlet*, Why Not has helped Birley build her own Deaf-centred company, 1S1, and supported multiple 1S1 productions including *Lady M*, a Deaf-hearing prequel to *MacBeth*, which premiered in Toronto in July 2023.

in-kind support from the Brighton Festival and sign-ons from several other companies as design and producing partners. Even then, there were no guarantees: after three weeks of rehearsal in Shoreham-on-Sea ahead of the show's premiere in May 2023, fractures emerged around what Frankland called, in an off-the-record chat with me in July 2023, "ideas of so-called professionalism,"[81] causing one of *Galatea*'s directors to step away. This left Frankland, Subira Joy, Kesson, and other artistic leaders scrambling to ensure safety and continuity. The production was then hit by a new challenge, a long-term incursion onto the performance site that put its insurance cover in jeopardy. To manage these difficulties, a three-week run had to be cut to one week, though the resulting show was extremely well received by many audience members (as evidenced by Kesson's research team's exit surveys and discussions, shared with me anecdotally).

The precarity of the funding structure that made a full-scale *Galatea* possible almost tore it apart in the end. Why? Because the work of democratizing story is twofold: it is the work of establishing and funding the necessity of full access to the making and sharing of story, and it is *also* the work of mounting that story for a paying audience in a culture still driven by "European standards of excellence" – standards that still have a tenacious hold on many of us in the industry who are nevertheless committed to real equity and inclusion. The work of democratizing story requires navigating this paradox, which means that it requires more than just *adequate* provision – it requires stable, significant money, space, time, and administrative aid, all offered without creative strings attached to the artists it supplies. This is the kind of support Why Not is in the business of making theatre to fund, and it is a major reason it continues to choose Shakespeare in its fight for a richer, less cis-, less white, less ableist, and more dynamic theatre ecology.[82] In Section 4, I'll explore how large Shakespeare institutions can follow Why Not's lead and do their part to provision artists like Emma Frankland – as a matter of mission and vision, not gift or charity.

4 Institutional Change

A company is a political act.

Ravi Jain[83]

Please, universe, let me be a ladder.

Nataki Garrett[84]

---

[81] While this discussion was informal, Frankland has given me her consent to include this attributed quotation here.
[82] M. Fernandes and R. Jain, personal interview, 7 December 2021.
[83] M. Fernandes and R. Jain, personal interview, 7 December 2021.
[84] N. Garrett, personal interview, 5 October 2022.

In early August 2020, deep into the first Covid-19 lockdown, Shakespeare's Globe (2020) released the sixth season of its podcast *Such Stuff*, focused on whiteness in and beyond the Shakespeare industry. The drop was timed to coincide with the Globe's third Shakespeare and Race conference. "With the theatre closed," reads the first episode lede, "we take a moment to ask: when we reopen, should we really go back to business as usual?" George Floyd's murder, Breonna Taylor's murder, and global Black Lives Matter uprisings dominated headlines that summer alongside the pandemic. Across the Anglophone theatre world, marquee companies were releasing statements of solidarity asking, "what is equity, *really*?" (Nataki Garrett, quoted in Doyle 2020, my emphasis). Then, in June 2021, a collective of US-based BIPOC theatre workers released *We See You, White American Theater* (n.d.). This gathering of documents contains a statement, a set of principles for developing "anti-racist theater systems," and a list of demands. Demands – not requests – for large-scale, long overdue, institutional change.

In this section, I examine institutional change in progress at two theatre companies dedicated to Shakespeare's legacy: Shakespeare's Globe in London, and the Oregon Shakespeare Festival (OSF) in Ashland, OR. Under the leadership of two prominent women artists committed to social justice and long-overdue racial uplift, can these theatres finally shift away from a model that centres Shakespeare as a pinnacle of colonially defined "excellence" and toward one that centres equity, *but really*? Can they stop relying on Shakespeare's cultural credentials for fundraising and ticket sales and move toward critical conversations about the racist power structures that continue to benefit from our deep, felt attachments to Shakespeare and his works? I begin with a brief discussion of "institutional Shakespeare" and its foundational relationship to "whiteness" to demonstrate how urgent not just feminist but properly *intersectional* change is to the work of decolonizing Shakespeare's legacy theatres. I then explore some of the key changes, especially around race, that have been taking place at Shakespeare's Globe, arguably the most prominent Shakespeare theatre in the world. These changes are a promising start, but they are also just that: a start. They aim for inclusion, to be sure, but they are not yet – as Dawn Jani Birley might note – properly intersectional or fully equitable. What might next steps look like? To help answer that question, I turn to the OSF and its first Black female artistic director, Nataki Garrett.

4.1 Shakespeare as an Institution

As Jen Harvie (2013), Christopher B. Balme (2017), Michael McKinnie (2021), and other scholars of the public sphere note, even at its most independent and intellectually progressive, the constellation of places, people, and ideas we call "the theatre" is always bound up in a web of institutions. These institutions include things like civic, regional, and national governments, universities, cultural granting agencies, and real estate markets, to name just a few. Theatre companies that own their buildings are especially embedded, both physically and philosophically, in the institutions that organize the spaces around them. They operate at the nexus of a wide range of stakeholders and their interests: their boards of directors, their audience subscription base, civic leaders and planners, donors and trusts, and government grant schemes. These institutional enmeshments all converge at market capitalism – the ultimate umbrella institution that prefers fiscal stability, moderate risk, and social and political status quos. This network of institutions holds the power to determine what moves toward systemic structural change a given theatre organization is willing, or even able, to undertake.

Within this landscape, theatres like the Globe, Ontario's Stratford Festival, and the RSC in Stratford-upon-Avon face a double bind. Market capitalism aside, they are also enmeshed in the web of socially, culturally, and racially inflected feelings about who Shakespeare is for (who "owns" Shakespeare, as I put it in Section 1) – feelings that form the basis of Shakespeare's status as a powerful economic mover. Bricks-and-mortar theatres rely heavily on their audience subscription bases for funding stability, and subscribers to legacy Shakespeare theatres trend affluent, older, and almost invariably white. They are there precisely because Shakespeare reflects back to them their own sense of self. Corporate donors – which can include banks, insurance companies, asset management firms, big tech, and more – feel the same pull as they use Shakespeare's elite cultural capital to burnish their brands. But this pull, as David Sterling Brown and Sandra Young write, is by no means racially neutral because "the Shakespeare industry is implicated in the colonialist habits of thought that shaped early modern culture and the racist inheritance that has continued to privilege whiteness and perpetuate anti-Black racism from early modernity to the present" (Brown and Young 2021, 531). When we "love" Shakespeare, what do we love about him or his work? When we see ourselves in Shakespeare, what do we see? These questions always have multiple answers, of course – and some of those answers can be profoundly empowering, as they have been for the artists I profiled in earlier sections. Other answers, though, can be challenging to face. In Shakespeare's own historical moment, what people loved about him, what they saw in him, was often their own desire *to be white*.

In his introduction to *White People in Shakespeare*, Arthur L. Little, Jr (2022) argues that Shakespeare's plays and poems "actively engage in 'white-people-making,'" while white people themselves "have used Shakespeare to define and bolster their white cultural racial identity, solidarity, and authority" since his works first appeared (Little 2022, 1). The cult of whiteness was everywhere in Shakespeare's England: from the court of Elizabeth I, to the religious fetish for "the soul's whiteness," to that concept's extension into secular humanist doctrine as "a privileged few linked their whiteness to the 'light' of knowledge within" (Little 2022, 5). Cheryl Harris writes that through the seventeenth century "Whiteness was the characteristic, the attribute, *the property of free human beings*" (quoted in Little 2022, 5, my emphasis). Whiteness was currency, a prized possession, traded as cultural capital; it increased one's social standing within a heterogeneous human landscape in a busy trading centre (London) at the birth of modern global capitalism. Early modern London's theatre ecology was a highly accessible, comparatively mixed public space in which actors and authors could perform whiteness as a core attribute and project it onto their audiences, challenging the exclusive claims to whiteness of the court and its elites. The central question of *who gets to claim to be white* is thus foundational to the work of Shakespeare and his contemporaries, is wrapped up in Shakespeare's marketability, and forms a central component of his elite status: "The theatre lit onstage English bodies, painted them [white], and discoursed about them to the point where those looking on could with confidence and pride imagine themselves to be 'white people,'" Little, Jr notes (Little 2022, 6). The early modern theatre sold "whiteness" as a value you needed and an attribute you wanted – just as modern Shakespeare theatres sell access to Shakespeare's social and cultural capital, the joy and pride of feeling like you are someone whom Shakespeare is "for."[85]

This set of tricky institutional circumstances creates a pernicious dilemma for theatres like Shakespeare's Globe and the OSF. Before anything else, decolonization for them must mean reckoning with the fact that your very reason for existing – to sell "elite whiteness" – is at the heart of the problem you're trying to solve. Ayanna Thompson puts the question well: "How do you create an equitable theater space [within a space] that was founded and structured in an inequitable way?" (Thompson, Karim-Cooper, and Brown 2021). The challenge, as we'll see, requires a wholesale rethinking of these theatres' business models – a prospect that is both terrifying and yet potentially liberating. It requires bringing existing, Shakespeare-attached audiences along while you deliberately question their attachments in productive, meaningful ways. It requires making space for equity-owed artists and equity-owed

---

[85] To muster just one example from Little Jr's extensive catalogue: "the word 'fair' occurs more than nine hundred times in [Shakespeare's] works, often in relationship to a woman's skin and beauty, and the word 'white' just under two hundred times, with many of those also referencing the 'natural' beauty of a woman's skin" (Little 2022, 7).

designers and crew specialists, and then finding the money and time to resource and support them as leaders – as central, not add-ons. Most of all, it requires a firm commitment to building *new* audiences from those constituencies never before invited to see themselves as part of Shakespeare's institutional universe.

4.2 "One Globe"

In November 2016, after just a few months in post, celebrated physical theatre director Emma Rice stepped down as artistic director of Shakespeare's Globe in what was widely reported as a dispute over her use of amplified sound and electric lighting. Rice had a different take: that her working-class status and her outspokenness about finding Shakespeare "difficult" were both factors that broke her relationship with the theatre's board of trustees (BBC Radio 2017; Brown 2017; Hemley 2017). Whatever the nuances of Rice's departure, losing a prominent, populist director in such a public way generated emotional upheaval as well as a reputational blow for a theatre company that believes that it was founded on democratic, knowledge-seeking principles and consistently claims that its mandate is to make Shakespeare available "for all" (Fowler and Solga in press).

Shakespeare's Globe was founded in 1997 as a place of contemporary academic research into historical performance conditions on London's South Bank. It has one of the most robust education and research mandates of any theatre in the Anglophone world, yet it earns no public subsidy; its revenue comes from box office, education, tour bookings, bookshop and restaurant sales, as well as donations and legacy gifts. This means that its research and education capacity, let alone its artistic programming, is always financially dependent on a mix of commercial appeal, market-driven circumstances, and individual taste. At the beginning, the Globe focused famously on "original practices" (OP): the material constraints (including costume, lighting, sound, architecture, the weather, male actors in all roles) that shaped the production of Shakespeare's plays in the original outdoor theatre. While the OP commitment was sidelined by the Globe's second artistic director, Dominic Dromgoole, in favour of a commitment to new writing by contemporary artists, the Globe was conceived and created as a true-to-historical-detail, reconstructed Elizabethan playhouse, and thus "original" playing conditions will always form a core part of its education and research programs, its artistic approaches, and its fiscal bottom line. As Research Fellow Will Tosh told me, a major problem with Emma Rice's innovations was the damage they risked doing to the "fabric of the building": if the physical space of the Globe's iconic theatre is altered permanently, the organization's larger research mandate, its educational capacity, its artistic appeal, and therefore its financial viability may become endangered.[86]

Shakespeare "for all" has long been the Globe's unofficial slogan, a clear echo of the idea of Shakespeare as a "universal" artist. At the same time, of course, Shakespeare's Globe is clearly *not* devoted to all – the clue is in the name. The Globe's "for all" is a prime example of what Dawn Jani Birley describes as the logic of "inclusion": all are welcome, but on the terms set by the institution. This is not to say that the Globe intends exclusivity, but the premise behind "inclusion" – that opening the doors to all simply equals accessibility for all – signals a lack of deep, lived understanding of what it takes to walk through an open door if you've never been invited. A prime example of "for all" at the Globe was the Globe2Globe Festival, which took place in 2012–13 as part of London's 2012 cultural Olympiad to showcase "one Globe" as a source of British pride in a multicultural, post-colonial landscape (see Solga 2013 and other essays in Bennett and Carson 2013). Yvette Nolan recalls being told that her *Julius Caesar* adaptation *Death of a Chief* could not qualify for the festival because it was in English, even though Nolan's company had chosen deliberately to work with Shakespeare's original text to serve their own needs as Indigenous artists (see Section 1). The exclusion – in the name of inclusion! – of *Death of a Chief* neatly represents what Elliot Barnes-Worrell described in a Globe panel discussion on race in August 2020: Black, Brown, Indigenous, and other global majority artists have been required "to go through whiteness" to be able to work at the Globe (Karim-Cooper et al. 2020).

The work of dismantling this barrier – having to "go through" whiteness, normate ability, binary gender presentation, European expectations of "excellence," and more to walk through the Globe's open doors – has now begun in earnest. In mid 2017, Michelle Terry was named the Globe's incoming artistic director. Young, female, a frequent Globe performer, and an unabashed Shakespeare fan, Terry was an optically ideal replacement for Rice, yet quickly she proved herself anything but the expected "safe pair of hands."[87] First, she declared publicly that Rice's tenure had been "the best thing that has ever happened to the Globe" because it generated a "healthy form of protest" and opened space for much-needed "self reflection" (Bowie-Sell 2017). Second, she explained that her role at the Globe would be to widen access, "diversify the decision-makers," and use her own cultural capital as a celebrated Shakespearean actor to "put social justice on our stages" (Curtis 2019). Terry,

---

[86] W. Tosh, personal interview, 5 November 2021.
[87] W. Tosh, personal interview, 5 November 2021.

who trained as an actor rather than a director, opted to play the artistic director role as an actor-manager. She quickly created the Globe's first artistic council, a group of advisors made up of both artists familiar to the Globe and those who had not before worked (or had not been invited to work) at the theatre. The council advises Terry directly and operates as "part of the governance structure but not beholden to [it]";[88] the council thus allows Terry to take unmediated and multi-perspectival artist feedback directly to the theatre's chief executive officer (CEO) and board of trustees. It balances the relative lack of artistic experience at trustee level and interrupts the senior leadership team's market-driven thinking with a nuanced understanding of the larger value of taking "artistic risks" with the public good in mind.

Terry's early initiatives – including some very bold programming choices, such as Morgan Lloyd Malcolm's *Emilia*, Marlowe's *Edward II*, *After Edward*, which was created by and for the cast of *Edward II*, and Andoh and Linton's *Richard II* (see below) – directly targeted the existing logic of "for all," both backstage and onstage, but they did not occur in a vacuum. Long before Rice's departure, Globe head of research Farah Karim-Cooper had been pressing questions of race, access, and social justice as the lone person of colour on the senior leadership team. Karim-Cooper's capacity to challenge status quos at the Globe derives in part from her separate academic appointment at King's College London, which grants her significant autonomy, and in part from her prominent and respected position as a scholar within the academic Shakespeare industry. (Here we should note parallels with Kesson's work on *Galatea*, which includes significant material support, and Sorouja Moll's on *1939*. Scholars can and should be a major resource for artists in the process of decolonizing Shakespeare and his spaces.) In the mid 2010s, Karim-Cooper made the decision to pivot her academic research directly toward issues of race, bringing "the [Globe] institution along with her" (Thompson, Karim-Cooper, and Brown 2021, 540). While this work was ongoing, Rice's departure in late 2016 raised urgent questions about who exactly counts as "for all" under the Globe's banner of broad inclusivity; conversations ensued inside the organization about intersectionality and large-scale diversification at all artistic and leadership levels. Finally, in April 2018, after an external governance review, the Globe undertook a restructuring that placed Terry, as incoming artistic director, in a horizontal leadership band including co-directors of education Karim-Cooper and Lucy Cuthbertson, co-directors of development Amy Cody and Charlotte Wren, finance director Joel Moseley, and director of audiences Becky Wooton (all as of January 2023). This reorientation challenges the vertical hierarchy model of

---

[88] M. Terry, personal interview, 19 January 2022.

most repertory theatres (artistic director; associate artistic directors; producers; and so on down the line), imbricating all directors in one another's initiatives, and in theory aligns the organization's overarching commitment to social justice. In practice, it has led to publicly visible leadership sharing between Terry and Karim-Cooper on the latter's high-profile anti-racism initiatives. These include the now-annual Shakespeare and Race conference, the ongoing Anti-Racist Shakespeare webinar series that curates race-conscious conversations about each play in the theatre season, social media advocacy, leadership on the Globe's anti-racism task force, and season 6 of the podcast *Such Stuff* (Shakespeare's Globe 2020).

From outside, the Globe's decolonial future looks rosy; however, the truth is often more complicated. Karim-Cooper noted in early 2021 that much of the Globe's current capacity on anti-racism comes from pressure she exerts; as an outspoken and resourced leader of colour, she has both the space and the motivation to keep those issues top of mind. "If I left tomorrow, I'd be worried about how they'd proceed with this mission," she notes (Thompson, Karim-Cooper, and Brown 2021, 539), exposing how much equity work relies on the labour and commitment of individual stakeholders from equity-owed communities, taxing their resources and risking burnout. Karim-Cooper's experience represents an example of the "benevolence" or "charity" model of change, in which "equity" is seen as something that organizations "give" to Black people, disabled people, or trans people, rather than as something that must be built and sustained by all hands for the organization's and its communities' own future good (Morgan et al. 2019). The risk that theatres like Shakespeare's Globe will remain mired in a benevolence model, rather than undertaking further, expensive systemic change to support intersectional equity, has only increased as the Covid-19 pandemic and its aftermath left many theatres on the economic brink, with travel uncertain and expensive, and subscriber numbers dwindling (Paulson 2023).

What does "benevolent" equity look like in practice? In 2017 Michelle Terry commissioned Adjua Andoh to create *Richard II* for the Sam Wanamaker playhouse. Andoh and her co-director Lynette Linton conceived their *Richard II* as a response to Windrush, to Brexit, and to surging white supremacy in the UK. An all woman-of-colour production, from cast and creative team to backstage, photography, marketing, and more, its goal was to perform received history – English history, Shakespeare's history – through the voices and experiences of the women "at the bottom of [the empire's] heap" (*Such Stuff* podcast, Shakespeare's Globe 2020). "[Andoh] walked into the [Wanamaker theatre], and she was like, 'This is the space of empire. We're going to change that,'" Karim-Cooper says, noting how much she and others on the leadership team learned from working with Andoh (Thompson, Karim-Cooper, and Brown 2021, 551). Terry's platforming of Andoh and Linton's project was a major step forward for the Globe, but actually renovating the "space of empire" requires a lot more than goodwill and intention. It takes incredible work – work that ultimately fell to Linton and Andoh. The Globe's back of house didn't have a Rolodex of Black female artisans and crew at the ready and didn't know where to look; Andoh and Linton plugged the gap and advocated for better. It was their authority as Black women theatre leaders and their being willing, like Karim-Cooper, to call the organization out (including publicly), to press hard for the support they needed, and to muster further resources that ultimately allowed the show to stand on its feet. One of Andoh's conditions for the commission was that *Richard II* would be an invitation to "people who might not have come to the Globe before" (Jackson 2019). Her goal was audience development: to bring the women and others "at the bottom [of the empire's] heap" into the emperor's house, to let them see themselves and each other *belonging there*. She decided that the production needed to be filmed and widely disseminated; to make that happen, Andoh set up her own production company. The Globe has robust film resources in its in-house, fee-charging Globe Player, but it chose not to platform *Richard II* that way. The film was made independently by Andoh's company and remains available free of charge – on YouTube.[89]

Michelle Terry provided Andoh and Linton with a high-profile and iconic space in which to tell Shakespeare's history not as a universal story but as *their* story; in turn, the artists illuminated how much the Globe's internal working structures continue to privilege certain bodies, identities, and experiences over others. They revealed what needs still to change at the Globe, and how much work that change will take. If a building isn't intentionally built by or for equity-owed people, it probably can't imagine what it will take for those people to feel comfortable and safe working there, to feel "at home" there, let alone to feel able to *lead* there (Nataki Garrett, in Doyle 2020).[90] Lasting institutional change in the Shakespeare industry can't come from structures as usual; it will only emerge from a critical mass of diverse lived experiences inside organizations, coupled with a strong scaffold on which to hold, grow, and develop their talents and leadership skills. What "equity, really" needs is artistic leaders who are willing to use all of their resources to become "a ladder" for the talented but

---

[89] See it at www.youtube.com/watch?v=BHrXAJ93hRU.

[90] Andoh speaks powerfully about this issue in her contribution to *Such Stuff*, Season 6, Episode 4 (Shakespeare's Globe 2020): "if you looked at the make-up of the people on stage and you look at the make-up of the people backstage, or in the back offices, or in the decision-making parts of the building, the heads of departments . . . you will find that they will struggle to reflect what is . . . on stage and that dissonance is a problem."

hugely under-resourced women of difference coming up behind them – and then to get out of their way (Oregon Art Beat 2021; Thompson, Karim-Cooper, and Brown 2021, 552).

4.3 Becoming a Ladder

EVERYTHING has to shift.

Nataki Garrett[91]

Nataki Garrett was raised in Oakland, California, by a family that showed her, every day, her worth, strength, and responsibility as a young Black woman. Her parents were "revolutionaries"; her grandmother was a ballerina who told her she would become a theatre director one day (Smith 2021). Her family was working class but educated; they lacked the economic resources of many of their middle-class peers, but they had knowledge, they had deep cultural roots in both Black American culture and the broader arts landscape, and they held within their community a powerful history of civil rights activism. "I come from a family of organizers – seeing them create spaces to enfranchise people got in my blood," Garrett notes (Chávez 2020).

Like the other women I profile in this Element, Garrett had an early, formative experience with Shakespeare that made him her collaborator and ally, not a superior or a threat. In seventh grade, her class explored *Romeo and Juliet*; her teacher invited everyone to "respond artistically in whatever way we wanted."[92] Garrett wrote a poem; others created dance. The experience stuck: "Any other Shakespeare I read after that I felt like it belonged to me, like it was mine. I was *supposed* to read it. I was *supposed* to understand it. I was supposed to be connected to the language. I wasn't supposed to be intimidated by it."[93] Once she got to high school, the message changed. In English class she was steered away from playing Viola or Julius Caesar and toward Emilia or Juliet's Nurse. She turned away from Shakespeare in scene study. She experienced similar pushback in grad school: during her master of fine arts (MFA) at CalArts, she chose to direct *The Duchess of Malfi* but was "curtail[ed]" by the program, which wanted her to work on an African American text to "capitalize" on her existing, perceived strengths as a young Black radical. Garrett wanted to work on a classic play precisely because she knew that "nobody is ever going to ask me to direct any classical text professionally in the world." She received less money for her *Malfi* than previous student directors using the same space had

---

[91] N. Garrett, personal interview, 5 October 2022.

[92] N. Garrett, personal interview, 5 October 2022.

[93] N. Garrett, personal interview, 5 October 2022. Emphasis in original.

been given, and she was denied her first choice of actors. Her teachers wanted her to fit into a box, to be the "other" they recognized; she refused.[94]

Garrett went on to become not just an award-winning director but a professor, an associate dean and associate artistic director at CalArts, and then a leader at the Denver Center. When the opportunity came up to apply for the artistic directorship at the OSF, she knew two things: that there was "no way" the OSF, one of the largest public theatres in the US, was going to hire her; and that she couldn't "not apply." The process was not an easy one; the OSF's then board of directors tried at every turn to find reasons not to hire her, she says, including calling multiple former co-workers at the Denver Center, some more than once. "What I heard after the fact is that in the process of my applying and all of my interviews, there was really just no denying that I was the candidate," she reflected to me. Once that fact was clear, the board worked overtime to find "a reason either to substantiate that I should be hired or for me not to be hired."[95]

Garrett's experience with the OSF board's excessive diligence was just the beginning. Oregon is stereotyped as a super-woke place, but it was "founded with a racial exclusion clause in its constitution ... unfair labor laws for migrants ... and an active KKK presence well into the 20th if not the 21st century" (Qureshi 2022). Today, Ashland, the OSF's rural southern Oregon home, is 90 per cent white and a place where the OSF's BIPOC artists are routinely harassed by residents and the police (Qureshi 2022).[96] During her tenure at the OSF (which ended in May 2023; see Section 5), Garrett travelled with a security detail and she and other OSF team members dealt with death threats; her changes at the festival, she recognized, generated significant outrage from those who felt that something "important to them ... is being taken away" (Qureshi 2022). She told me that had she known what the experience of actually leading the OSF on the ground would be, she might not have taken the job; yet she came because the OSF was a company already on a path to change, and one she knew she had the skills to transform. Her sense of her responsibility to her community played a role, too: "How do I make sure that there's a generation of people who come behind me who are like, 'listen, I'm here because you were a ladder'?" (Oregon Art Beat 2021).

Like the Globe does today, the OSF has long identified as a "social justice theatre."[97] But how do you turn a "social justice theatre" into an anti-racist theatre? As Garrett describes it, the OSF had already "set itself on a path to shift culture" under former artistic director Bill Rauch (2007–19), becoming what

---

[94] N. Garrett, personal interview, 5 October 2022.
[95] N. Garrett, personal interview, 5 October 2022.
[96] N. Garrett, personal interview, 5 October 2022.
[97] N. Garrett, personal interview, 5 October 2022.

she describes as a model for equity and diversity "across the theatrical land-scape" (Morgan et al. 2019). However, "what [had] not shifted" was the attitude of "benevolence" I explored a little earlier: "'We gave you a seat at the table, now don't ruin it,'" she notes of those who hired her, "as though it was their table to give" (Morgan et al. 2019). To make the shift from "benevolence" to "equity, really," Garrett developed a strategy of total systems change across every aspect of the 600-person strong OSF operation. Her strategy involved placing artists, their goals, and their needs at the heart of everything the OSF does; completely reorganizing the company's administrative and fundraising systems to lessen the fear that "change" will result in bankruptcy; and changing the terms of audience engagement to "desegregate the other side of the foot-lights" (Morgan et al. 2019), widening spectatorship across a new digital platform and via other outreach tools. Garrett recalls learning, years into adulthood, that her Bay Area high school ran an informal annual trip to the OSF; she was never invited to go, her friends thinking she wouldn't be inter-ested (NEA 2021). Shifting the OSF's centre meant, for Garrett, fundamentally addressing that ownership gap: the one that wrote her out of Shakespeare without her even knowing, the one that could not even *imagine* a body like hers in the audience.

Garrett's artist-first approach derives from her practice as a director. "I actually walk into any rehearsal space with the understanding that the world of the play already lives inside of the actor," she explains; especially when she's working with artists who are used to being instrumentalized by direct-ors, she "takes [tiny steps] to get an artist to a place where they feel like they can trust themselves and they can trust the emotion and they can trust ... their own point of view."[98] Her job in the room, she tells me, is to "free the story forward": when scaled up, this approach "create[s] a space for artists where they can respond to a multiplicity of impulses through whatever modality they want." Like Emma Frankland, Garrett sees her role as holding space and mustering resources so that her artists can concentrate on making, not on chasing logistical details that should be a central, institutional respon-sibility. For example, theatre and virtual reality maker Shariffa Ali came to the OSF on a theatre residency, and then realized she wanted to make a film. Garrett moved money around to enable Ali's modality shift, and the result was *ASH LAND*, a piece about Black female healing, joy, and embodiment that helped launch *O!*, the OSF's new digital doorway. Garrett "gave her a residency and she created a film company out of it" (Smith 2021); the contrast with Andoh's experience at the Globe is instructive.

---

[98] N. Garrett, personal interview, 5 October 2022.

Garrett purposefully met Ali at "the intersection between what is important to you and what is important to us," but then she asked a key question: "How do we bring those things together? How do we work together to create that space?" (Morgan et al. 2019).

Labour considerations lie at the heart of this artist-forward strategy; they also power the administrative changes Garrett made at the OSF. She leaned hard into fundraising as the best way she could resource the artists she wanted to uplift while bringing the company's economic base with her. She arrived at the OSF an already strong fundraiser, and during the first six months of the Covid-19 pandemic she raised USD 6 million for the company and collaborated with other Oregon arts leaders to secure a further USD 8 million pandemic relief package (Doyle 2020; Taylor 2021). She flattened the OSF's executive leadership structure to create a band including three associate directors (artistic programming; innovation and strategy; new work) alongside the existing director of production and a new director of inclusion, equity, diversity, and accessibility (IDEA); the leadership core also includes a director of audience experience and a director of development. As at the Globe, this horizontal structure creates tremendous opportunities for cross-pollination, but it also creates much more humane working conditions for all. "I needed a team in which I had no single point of failure and in which everybody could produce everybody else's work," Garrett explained to me.[99] A team of equals ensures that the company community always has its members' backs.

Garrett also expanded the long-held notion (since Libby Appel's tenure as artistic director, 1995–2007) of the OSF as a "home" for its resident acting company, widening that concept so that "home" becomes known as a secure place from which artists can explore and grow within but also beyond Ashland. This home, in her words, is "not a club," which "is a private space that excludes people," but rather a place where "a lot of people can be connected" (Doyle 2020). The OSF as "home" stretches the length of the coast from Seattle to San Francisco; Garrett worked with regional sister companies to develop opportunities for company members, allowing them to work throughout the year while also remaining based at the OSF. Her company-as-home model mirrors the strength she draws from fellow members of what she calls the "movement" currently underway to shift American theatre leadership at the topmost levels; as one of several high-profile artistic directors of colour newly in role circa 2021 (including Hana Sharif, Jacob Padrón, Eric Ting, and prominent industry leaders like Carmen Morgan at artsEquity, an OSF producing partner), Garrett is quick to point out that she is only one member of a growing, internally

---

[99] N. Garrett, personal interview, 5 October 2022.

sustaining, activist BIPOC theatre community – a BIPOC theatre activist in the heart of Shakespeare country.

Garrett's artist-centred approach also centres access and engagement on the other side of the footlights; for her, shifting the OSF's culture also meant moving away from the traditional subscription model and the "exclusivized experience" it sells – that felt sense that this show "belongs to me," where "me" is a specific group of middle-class white folks (Morgan et al. 2019). The pull of audience ownership at the OSF, as at similar institutions, drives season selection but also para-theatrical programming, as well as donor and grant support. The OSF has long held grants to diversify its audiences, but the logic behind those moves has historically been something Garrett describes as "additive": "The [grant application] does not say what we're doing is creating a space in which there's equality at the centre. We said we're centring this group of people [existing subscribers] and then these people [BIPOC or equity-owed spectators] can be additive."[100] Garrett's most significant innovation at the OSF was spearheading the development of the company's digital platform, *O!*, which aims to make the OSF's audience base global as well as to widen access for local audience members who may experience mobility or financial constraints. Since *O!* received a boost from the Covid-19 pandemic's turn toward digital theatre, it has streamed born digital content such as *ASH LAND* (2020), *The Digital Sovereignty Project* (2021), and *The Cymbeline Project* (2022–3) as well as select mainstage productions; it includes a mix of paid content, free streaming, and trailers for live work on stage. As of early 2021, *O!* was reaching 58 countries, with 10,000 views a month.

All the work that the OSF did under Garrett's tenure was guided by the principles and demands of *We See You, White American Theatre* (n.d.); Garrett notes that it took the organization the better part of her first year in role to go through the collective's documents, identify what work had already been done, and assess what work remained. During that time, she experienced "a lot of avoidance" driven by the fear of costs from members of OSF's administration. Her response was blunt: "What can you afford not to do?" Diversity work is not charity; it is "a way of allowing our theaters to really thrive and meet our mandates, our missions," she explains (NEA 2021). And just as the shift from "benevolence" to "equity, really" is a long game, Garrett sees herself as one leader in a long line of future leaders at the OSF, one member of a growing movement to shift theatre's institutional centres. "It's not just about me. I'm the figurehead, you know? I'm the front person for the band," she told me in early 2022. "I think about the potential for shifting white supremacy culture at my

---

[100] N. Garrett, personal interview, 5 October 2022.

organization as a shifting mantel. I'm going to do my part, and somebody's going to do their part, and then behind them is somebody else" so that the OSF will eventually become a "historically white" rather than a "predominantly white" institution (Morgan et al. 2019).

Tom Cornford (2023) explains that directors operate "at the intersections of art and finance, organisation and creativity" (43): "a director's fundamental responsibility is to shape the social relations of theatre production" (44). The power to shape a theatre's culture and its relations of making is often bestowed on those who promise to make the least dramatic changes when change is warranted; diversification is wonderful, in theory. Hana Sharif notes that BIPOC leaders are frequently hired "with the expectation that we will revolutionize the financial structures of the theatre, that we will create new relevancy for our institutions, that we will solve systemic problems . . . and that we will do it without stepping fundamentally outside the box that our predecessors created" (Morgan et al. 2019). The difference between a "social justice theatre" and an anti-racist, equity-focused theatre can perhaps be marked by the difference between hiring someone familiar-feeling, with the hope that they move the dial just a little bit, and hiring someone unfamiliar, with a genuine willingness to be surprised at what movement is truly possible.

5 The Way Forward

The legacy of colonization has forced us to understand and see and hear in very specific ways. Everything is determined by how I see you. And how I can imagine where you can get to. [If] we can change the politics of the imagination, we'll then have more possibilities to dream about the kinds of processes required to facilitate this work. And the who and the what, and how it looks, and what it feels like . . . it should be beyond what I expect it to be.

Ravi Jain[101]

Just three weeks after I handed in the final draft of this Element, Nataki Garrett announced that she was leaving the OSF. She noted the multiple crises she'd had to navigate during her tenure: the Covid-19 pandemic and its outsized effect on a destination theatre like the OSF; the wildfires that increasingly plague Ashland as the climate emergency bites; and, by late 2022, a fiscal crisis threatening the OSF's very survival. Garrett did not dwell on the overt racism she and her young family endured while living in Ashland, including a letter-writing campaign from a group called the "old white guard," though doubtless the stress of living as a Black woman leader under blatant white supremacy in a small town

---

[101] M. Fernandes and R. Jain, personal interview, 7 December 2021.

took a huge toll. "You kind of have to get out before you burn out," she said (Weinert-Kendt 2023).

Garrett's departure came at a time when the OSF had launched an emergency fundraising drive, and both Diane Yu, chair of the OSF's board, and Garrett noted a key issue: some of the donors who provide tens or even hundreds of thousands of dollars a year to the Festival, and who are crucial for its sustainability, were walking away. The strain of Covid-19 lockdowns on the OSF's reserves and the uncertainty of future fire seasons of course affected those relationships, alongside industry-wide subscriber attrition (Paulson 2023; Weinert-Kendt 2023). But the spectre of Garrett's race and her commitment to anti-racism at the OSF also played a major role. Garrett was blunt with me in early 2022 as she talked about the challenges of having to convince her board that she, a Black woman, could raise money; in 2023, she shared publicly that a major donor had told her, early in her tenure, that *she* was the reason that donor was pulling their funding. "'I want to make sure you know it's not because you're Black," this donor was careful to say, "but there are things about the organization that you just don't understand, and you have big shoes to fill" (Weinert-Kendt 2023).

The organization; *my* organization. *You just don't understand.* You don't fit here; your feet, your *body*, does not fit here.

All the artists I've profiled in this Element share a core commitment to uplift the next generation of makers; the stories I've told demonstrate how Nataki Garrett's metaphor of the ladder becomes real. Jani Lauzon, Yvette Nolan, and Reneltta Arluk authorize their Indigenous community members as both tellers and owners of their stories, deploying Shakespeare's big energy and using institutional funding creatively to redistribute power. Adjua Andoh and Lynette Linton use industry capital to advocate for the resources needed to properly reveal their performers in their own power, and to make their work freely, widely available online. Ravi Jain, Miriam Fernandes, and Christine Horne all throw out their plans to start again when they realize their stories don't suit the bodies in the room. These artists show us that to become a ladder is to decentre yourself, to recognize that your experience is in no way universal, and then to do everything you can to create the material conditions needed for other bodies and their experiences to take centre stage. In Birley's words: "I will never understand what it's like to be Black; a hearing Black person will never know what it's like to be Deaf . . . Where I have privilege, I can work with you to uplift you, and where you have privilege you can uplift me. This is a reciprocal relationship."[102]

---

[102] D. Jani Birley and C. Horne, personal interview, 7 March 2022.

Nataki Garrett's resignation from the OSF reminds us that structural change in the Shakespeare industry is still a radical prospect to many because it is above all an *expensive* prospect for those who have traditionally benefited from Shakespeare's cultural capital. The systemic conditions – English exceptionalism and colonial expansion, white supremacy, market capitalism – that enable one specific version of our early modern story to be told, and one group of owners to cleave to that story, are hard to shift because the economy of the Shakespeare industry fundamentally resists the logic of uplift, which requires decentring its core asset. The departure of Garrett from the OSF in May 2023, alongside the challenges that Frankland and her team faced that very same month mounting *Galatea* on the other side of the Atlantic, remind us that the work of uplift is ongoing, that it cannot work with business-as-usual, and that it is work for all of us to do. Every maker in the chain must be a rung in the ladder; the intersection is only safe when we're all standing in it together.

A new economy of uplift, a true Shakespearean gift economy, will be built by artistic leaders from equity-owed communities like Lauzon, Nolan, Arluk, Frankland, and Andoh, but also by leaders with forward-thinking visions for new resourcing and funding models, like Jain and Garrett. It must include artistic leaders of theatres with deep pockets, like Michelle Terry, and it will rely too on academic leaders and allies like Andy Kesson and Farah Karim-Cooper. Most of all it includes audience members. We buy tickets; our interests affect programming, propel donor buy-in, shape the risks that historically risk-averse theatres are willing to take. Audience members are programming leaders; we have incredible power to say whose imagination should become a reality, what worlds we want to see on stage. Now is the time for spectators who want to see Shakespeare for all, *but really*, to make our voices heard.

References

1939. (2022). [performance]. Stratford Festival, Stratford, ON.

Andoh, A. (2021). Directing *Richard II*: Adjoa Andoh in Conversation With Varsha Panjwani. In D. Jarrett-Macauley, E. McHugh and V. Panjwani – with A. Andoh and D. Croll, *Richard II* at Shakespeare's Globe 2019: A Collective Perspective. *Otherness: Essays and Studies*, 8(2), 13–31, at 19–24. https://bit.ly/3P41UiA.

Balme, C. B. (2017). *The Theatrical Public Sphere*. Cambridge: Cambridge University Press.

BBC Radio. (14 December 2017). *Front Row: Emma Rice, John Boyega, Laura Ingalls Wilder*. [online] BBC, www.bbc.co.uk/programmes/b09hp2sz [accessed 27 March 2023].

Bennett, S., and Carson, C. (2013). *Shakespeare Beyond English*. Cambridge: Cambridge University Press.

Bowie-Sell, D. (18 August 2017). Michelle Terry: "I Won't Be Directing While at Shakespeare's Globe." [online] *WhatsOnStage*, https://bit.ly/3UXhzE7 [accessed 27 March 2023].

Brown, D. S., and Young, S. (2021). (Un)Just Acts: Shakespeare and Social Justice in Contemporary Performance. *Shakespeare Bulletin*, 39(4), 529–35.

Brown, M. (19 April 2017). Shakespeare's Globe Board Did Not Respect Me, Says Artistic Director. [online] *Guardian*, https://bit.ly/3TjIRTI [accessed 16 January 2022].

Canada Council for the Arts. (2017). *New Chapter*. [online] Canada Council for the Arts, https://canadacouncil.ca/initiatives/new-chapter.

Carastathis, A. (2016). *Intersectionality: Origins, Contestations, Horizons*. Lincoln: University of Nebraska Press.

Catanese, B. W. (2011). *The Problem of the Color[blind]*. Ann Arbor: University of Michigan Press.

Chávez, D. J. (7 October 2020). Taking the Heat, and Leading Through Crises, at Oregon Shakes. [online] *American Theatre*, https://rb.gy/c6m2lb [accessed 3 March 2024].

Cockett, P., and Gough, M., eds. (in press). *Gender on the Transnational Early Modern Stage, Then and Now: A Performance as Research Approach*. Toronto: University of Toronto Press.

Cornford, T. (2023). Directors: Organisation, Authorship and Social Production. In J. Harvie and D. Rebellato, eds., *The Cambridge Companion to British Theatre since 1945*. Cambridge: Cambridge University Press, pp. 42–60.

Crenshaw, K. (1989). Demarginalizing the Intersection of Race and Sex: A Black Feminist Critique of Antidiscrimination Doctrine, Feminist Theory and Antiracist Politics. *University of Chicago Legal Forum*, 1(8), 139–67.

Curtis, N. (12 July 2019). Michelle Terry Interview: "There's No Hope Unless We Put Social Justice on Our Stages." [online] *Evening Standard*, https://rb.gy/tpsis9 [accessed 3 March 2024].

Davies, C. (10 December 2018). Engendering Before Shakespeare: Women and Early English Playhouse Ownership. [online] *Before Shakespeare*, https://rb.gy/ghw5k7 [accessed 29 March 2023].

Davies, C. (in press). The PaRchive: Archiving Process in Practice-as-Research and the Work of Theatre History. In P. Cockett and M. Gough, eds., *Gender on the Transnational Early Modern Stage, Then and Now: A Performance as Research Approach*. Toronto: University of Toronto Press.

Doyle, J. (2020). Classic Conversations with Nataki Garrett. [online video clip] *Classic Conversations*, www.youtube.com/watch?v=dKmR1n9KeqA [accessed 27 March 2023].

Erickson, P., and Hall, K. F., eds. (2016). Special Issue: Rereading Early Modern Race. *Shakespeare Quarterly*, 67(1).

Fitzpatrick, K. (2021). *Generous Thinking: A Radical Approach to Saving the University*. Baltimore, MD: Johns Hopkins University Press.

Fowler, B., and Solga, K. (in press). Equity, Inclusion, Intersectionality, and the Institution: Holding Change in Tension at the Bush and the Globe. In A. Awo-Mana, C. Canning, and N. Anan, eds., *The Routledge Companion to Feminist Performance*. London: Routledge.

Frankland, E. (2019a). *None of Us Is Yet a Robot: Five Performances on Gender Identity and the Politics of Transition*. London: Oberon Books.

Frankland, E. (2019b). Trans Women on Stage: Erasure, Resurgence and #notadebate. In J. Sewell and C. Smout, eds., *The Palgrave Handbook of the History of Women on Stage*. London: Palgrave, pp. 775–805.

Frankland, E., and Joy, S., adapters (2023). *Galatea*. By John Lyly. Ed. Andy Kesson. London: Methuen.

Frankland, E., and Kesson, A. (2019). "Perhaps John Lyly Was a Trans Woman?": An Interview about Performing Galatea's Queer, Transgender Stories. *Journal for Early Modern Cultural Studies*, 19(4), 284–98.

Hall, K. F. (1996). *Things of Darkness: Economies of Race and Gender in Early Modern England*. Ithaca, NY: Cornell University Press.

Hartley, A., Dunn, K., and Berry, C. (2021). Pedagogy: Decolonizing Shakespeare on Stage. In P. Kirwan and K. Prince, eds., *The Arden Research Handbook of Shakespeare and Contemporary Performance*. London: Bloomsbury, pp. 171–91.

Harvey, D. (2005). *A Brief History of Neoliberalism*. Oxford: Oxford University Press.

Harvie, J. (2013). *Fair Play: Art, Performance and Neoliberalism*. Basingstoke: Palgrave.

Hemley, M. (15 December 2017). Emma Rice: "My Working-Class Background Was a Barrier at the Globe." [online] *The Stage*, https://rb.gy/zne7eb [accessed 27 March 2023].

Jackson, S. (2019). Adjoa Andoh and Lynette Linton – Interview. [online] *Afridiziak Theatre News*, www.afridiziak.com/interviews/adjoa-andoh-and-lynette-linton/ [accessed 27 March 2023].

Julian, E., and Solga, K. (2021). Ethics: The Challenge of Practising (and Not Just Representing) Diversity at the Stratford Festival of Canada. In P. Kirwan and K. Prince, eds., *The Arden Research Handbook of Shakespeare and Contemporary Performance*. London: Bloomsbury, pp. 192–210.

Karim-Cooper, F. (2023). *The Great White Bard*. New York: Penguin.

Karim-Cooper, F., Taneja, P., Finn, M., and Barnes-Worrell, E. (2020). In Conversation: Reckoning With Our Past. [online video clip] *Shakespeare and Race Conference 2020*, www.youtube.com/watch?v=bVpIXgyGXXc [accessed 27 March 2023].

Kemp, S. (2019). Transgender Shakespeare Performance: A Holistic Dramaturgy. *Journal for Early Modern Cultural Studies*, 19(4), 265–83.

Knowles, R. (1995). From Nationalist to Multinational: The Stratford Festival, Free Trade, and the Discourses of Intercultural Tourism. *Theatre Journal*, 47(1), 19–41.

Knowles, R. (2004). *Reading the Material Theatre*. Cambridge: Cambridge University Press.

Knowles, R. (2007). Watching for Adaptation; or, How I Learned to Stop Worrying and Love the Bard. *Shakespeare Bulletin*, 25(3), 53–65.

Lauzon, J. (2016). The Search for Spiritual Transformation in Contemporary Theatre Practice. In Y. Nolan and R. Knowles, eds., *Performing Indignity*. Toronto: Playwrights Canada Press, pp. 87–97.

Lauzon, J., Moll, S., and Riordan, K. (2022). Indigenous Speakers Series Presents Jani Lauzon & Kaitlyn Riordan. [online video clip] University of Waterloo, www.youtube.com/watch?v=tmgATuUI5RI [accessed 27 March 2023].

Linton, L., and Andoh, A. dirs. (2019). *Richard II* . [online performance]. Swinging the Lens, www.youtube.com/watch?v=BHrXAJ93hRU [accessed 3 March 2024].

Little, Jr, A. L. (2022). *White People in Shakespeare: Essays on Race, Culture and the Elite*. London: Bloomsbury.

Loomba, A. (2002). *Shakespeare, Race, and Colonialism*. Oxford: Oxford University Press.

Loomba, A., and Orkin, M. (1998). *Post-Colonial Shakespeares*. Hoboken, NJ: Taylor and Francis.

Loughran, K. (in press). The Meeting of Art and Academia. In P. Cockett and M. Gough, eds., *Gender on the Transnational Early Modern Stage, Then and Now: A Performance as Research Approach*. Toronto: University of Toronto Press.

Manitowabi, S. (2018). The Seven Grandfather Teachings. [online] E-Campus Ontario, https://ecampusontario.pressbooks.pub/movementtowardsreconci liation/chapter/the-seven-grandfather-teachings/ [accessed 27 March 2023].

McKinnie, M. (2021). *Theatre in Market Economies*. Cambridge: Cambridge University Press.

Mitchell, K. and Rebellato, D. (2011). *A Woman Killed With Kindness: Platform Discussion with Katie Mitchell*. National Theatre, London. (Archival recording accessible at the NT digital archive on the Cut in London.)

Moll, S. (2006). Death of a Chief: An Interview with Yvette Nolan. *Canadian Shakespeares*. https://bit.ly/3J0VRbb.

Moreno, B. (2020). *Pawâkan Macbeth – A Cree Takeover*. [online] Edify Edmonton, https://edifyedmonton.com/active/things-to-do-active/pawakan-macbeth-a-cree-takeover/ [accessed 27 March 2023].

Morgan, C., Garrett, N., Padrón, J. G., Sharif, H., and Ting, E. (2019). *Talking Back: BIPOC Leaders*. [online] Art Equity, www.artequity.org/tb-bipoc-lead ers [accessed 27 March 2023].

National Endowment for the Arts (NEA). (12 March 2021). Nataki Garrett. [online podcast] *NEA Art Works*, www.arts.gov/stories/podcast/nataki-gar rett [accessed 27 March 2023].

Nolan, Y. (2014). What We Talk About When We Talk About Indian. In H. Gilbert and C. Gleghorn, *Recasting Commodity and Spectacle in the Indigenous Americas*. London: Institute of Latin American Studies, School of Advanced Study, University of London, pp. 223–34.

Nolan, Y. (2015). *Medicine Shows: Indigenous Performance Culture*. Toronto: Playwrights Canada Press.

Ontario Performing Arts Presenting Network. (2021). *Indigenous Artist Spotlight: Akpik Theatre*. [online] Ontario Presents, https://ontariopresents .ca/blog/indigenous-artist-spotlight-akpik-theatre [accessed 27 March 2023].

Oregon Art Beat. (2021). *Breaking the Mold*, Season 23, Episode 1. [online] PBS, www.pbs.org/video/breaking-the-mold-6dsigh/ [accessed 27 March 2023].

Oxford English Dictionary (OED). (n.d.). Metaphor. [online] OED, www.oed .com [accessed 27 March 2023].

Parolin, P. (2009). "What Revels Are in Hand?": A Change of Direction at the Stratford Shakespeare Festival of Canada. *Shakespeare Quarterly*, 60(2), 197–224.

Paulson, M. (29 August 2023). Hitting Theater Hard: The Loss of Subscribers Who Went to Everything. [online] *New York Times*, www.nytimes.com/2023/08/29/theater/theater-subscribers-losses.html [accessed 26 September 2023].

Qureshi, B. (2022). Oregon Shakespeare Festival Focuses on Expansion – But Is Not Without Its Critics. [online] *NPR*, https://rb.gy/2dab6b [accessed 27 March 2023].

Robinson, D. (2020). *Hungry Listening: Resonant Theory for Indigenous Sound Studies*. Minneapolis: University of Minnesota Press.

Shakespeare, W. [1597/1599]. *Romeo and Juliet*. In B. Mowat, P. Werstine, M. Poston, and R. Niles, eds., *The Folger Shakespeare*. [online], Folger Shakespeare Library, https://folger.edu/explore/shakespeares-works/romeo-and-juliet/ [accessed 29 March 2023].

Shakespeare's Globe. (3 September 2020). #SuchStuff S6 E4: How Whiteness Dominates Our Theatres. [online podcast] *Such Stuff*, https://bit.ly/42ZJ9SW.

Smith, M. (2021). Molly's Salon: Nataki Garrett and Stephanie Handel. [online video clip] *Molly's Salon*, www.youtube.com/watch?v=Qe9lj-1aGzQ [accessed 27 March 2023].

Solga, K. (2013). Neo-liberal Pleasure, Global Responsibility and the South Sudan Cymbeline. In S. Bennett and C. Carson, eds., *Shakespeare Beyond English: A Global Experiment*. Cambridge: Cambridge University Press, pp. 101–9.

Solga, K. (2017). Shakespeare's Property Ladder: Women Directors and the Politics of Ownership. In J. C. Bulman, ed., *The Oxford Handbook of Shakespeare and Performance*. Oxford: Oxford University Press, pp. 104–21.

Taylor, R. (2021). Food for Thought: A Blackbone China Dinner and Discussion. [online video clip] *Food for Thought: Arts Activism & Technology*, www.youtube.com/watch?v=MssjoVAHNIM&t=6s [accessed 27 March 2023].

Thompson, A. (2011). *Passing Strange: Shakespeare, Race, and Contemporary America*. Oxford: Oxford University Press.

Thompson, A. (2021). *The Cambridge Companion to Shakespeare and Race*. Cambridge: Cambridge University Press.

Thompson, A., Karim-Cooper, F., and Brown, D. S. (2021). "Unicorns and Fairy Dust": Talking Shakespeare, Performance, and Social (In)Justice. *Shakespeare Bulletin*, 39(4), 537–58.

Tuck, E., and Yang, K. W. (2012). Decolonization Is Not a Metaphor. *Decolonization: Indigeneity, Education & Society*, 1(1), 1–40.

Tuhiwai Smith, L. ([1999] 2021). *Decolonizing Methodologies: Research and Indigenous Peoples*, 2nd ed. London: Zed Books.

We See You, White American Theatre (n.d.). *We See You W.A.T.* [online], We See You, Statement tab, www.weseeyouwat.com.

Weinert-Kendt, R. (5 May 2023). Nataki Garrett to Leave Oregon Shakes Amid Emergency Fund Drive. [online] *American Theater*, https://bit.ly/48CSpxQ [accessed 26 September 2023].

Why Not Theatre (n.d.a). *About*. [online]. Why Not Theatre, https://Why Not .theatre/about/ [accessed 27 March 2023].

Why Not Theatre (n.d.b). *Share*. [online]. Why Not Theatre, https://Why Not .theatre/share/ [accessed 27 March 2023].

Why Not Theatre (2017). *Prince Hamlet*. [performance]. The Theatre Centre, Toronto, ON.

Why Not Theatre (2019). *Prince Hamlet*. [performance]. Canadian Stage, Toronto, ON.

Why Not Theatre (2021a). *R&J*. [performance]. Stratford Festival, Stratford, ON.

Why Not Theatre (2021b). *R+J: Behind the Scenes*. [online] Facebook, www .facebook.com/StratfordFestival/videos/634409450812566/ [accessed 27 March 2023].

Williams, N. J. (2022). Incomplete Dramaturgies. *Shakespeare Bulletin*, 40(1), 1–22.

Worthen, W. B. (1997). *Shakespeare and the Authority of Performance*. Cambridge: Cambridge University Press.

Acknowledgements

My sincerest thanks to the artists who agreed to speak with me – sometimes at great length and on multiple occasions! – in order that I might share their stories in this Element. From our conversations I learned so much about the work ahead of us as we strive toward decolonization in our arts and culture spaces.

I'm immensely grateful to Emma Frankland and Andy Kesson for opening their *Galatea* R&D room to me in November 2022. Being present to that work was truly an honour.

This Element could not have been completed without the assistance of Dr Sheetala Bhat, whose own work on theatrical decolonization is breaking new paths in our shared academic and artistic spaces.

Finally, I'm grateful for financial and sabbatical support from the Faculty of Arts and Humanities, Western University.

Cambridge Elements ≡

Women Theatre Makers

About the Series
This innovative, inclusive series showcases women-identifying theatre makers from around the world. Expansive in chronological and geographical scope, the series encompasses practitioners from the late nineteenth century onwards and addresses a global, comprehensive range of creatives – from playwrights and performers to directors and designers.

Cambridge Elements ☰

Women Theatre Makers

Elements in the Series

Maya Rao and Indian Feminist Theatre
Bishnupriya Dutt

Xin Fengxia and the Transformation of China's Ping Opera
Siyuan Liu

Emma Rice's Feminist Acts of Love
Lisa Peck

Clean Break Theatre Company
Caoimhe McAvinchey, Sarah Bartley, Deborah Dean, and Anne-marie Greene

Women Making Shakespeare in the Twenty-First Century
Kim Solga

A full series listing is available at: www.cambridge.org/EWTM

Printed in the United States
by Baker & Taylor Publisher Services